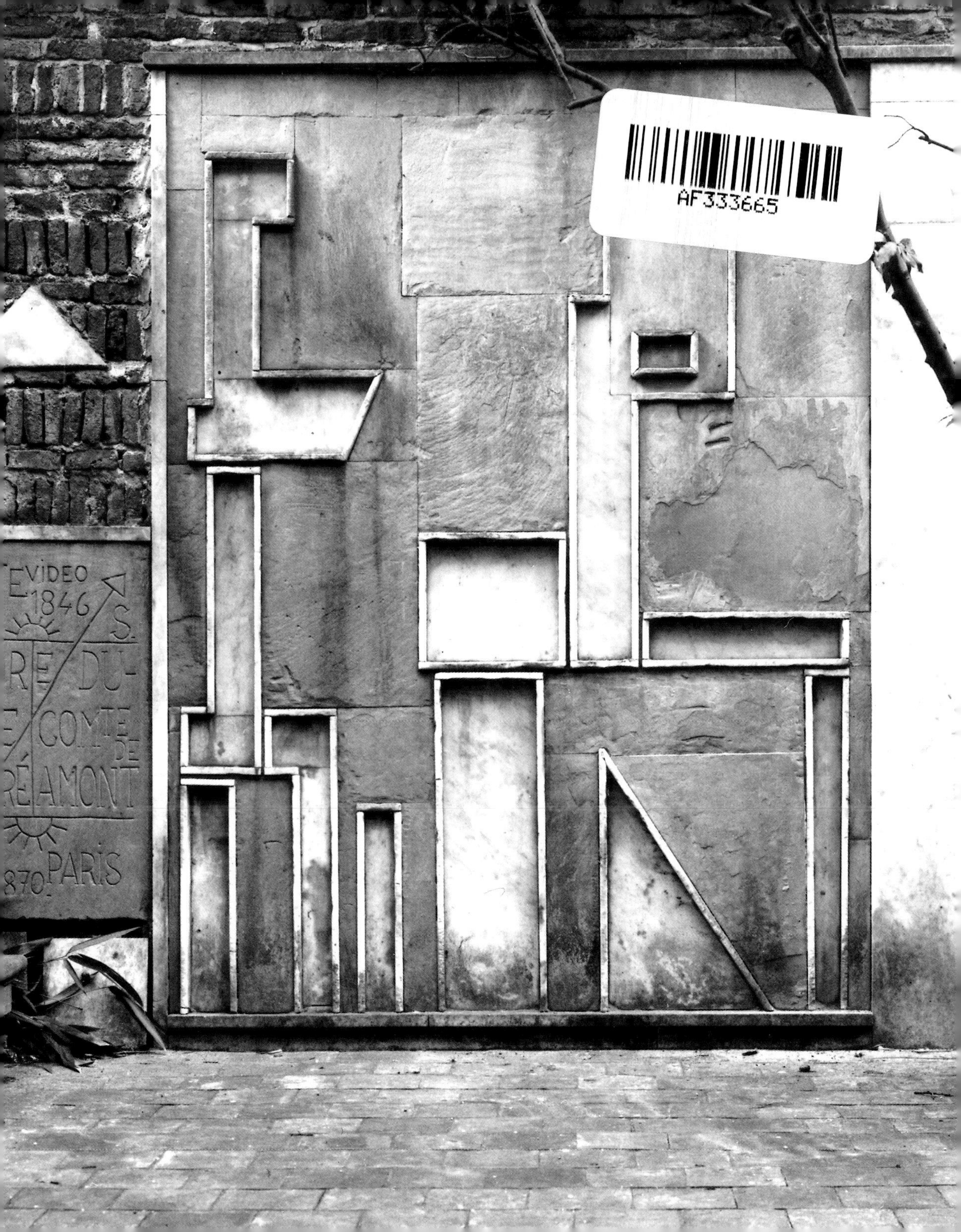
E VIDEO
1846
S.
RE DU
COMTE DE
RE AMONT
870. PARIS

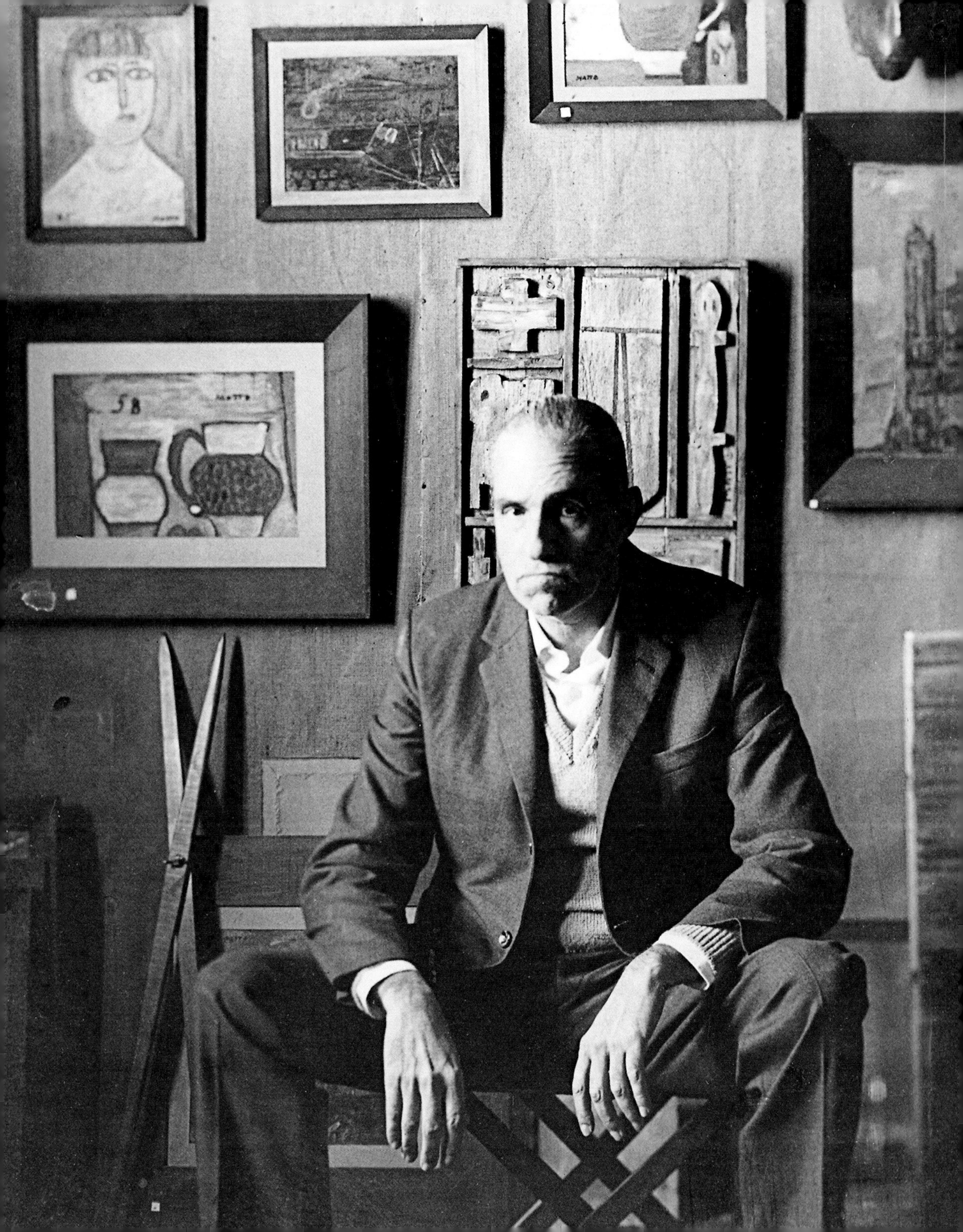

Francisco Matto
The Modern & the Mythic

EDITOR GABRIEL PÉREZ-BARREIRO
ESSAYS BY ROBERT C. MORGAN
AND CÉSAR PATERNOSTO

Blanton Museum of Art
The University of Texas at Austin

▨ The Blanton

Published by the Blanton Museum of Art, The University of Texas at Austin, on the occasion of the exhibition *Francisco Matto: The Modern and the Mythic*, June 21 to September 27, 2009.

Francisco Matto: The Modern and the Mythic was organized by the Blanton Museum of Art and adapted from its original presentation at the 6ª Bienal do Mercosul in Porto Alegre, Brazil.

Major support for the exhibition was provided by Judy and Charles Tate and the Susan Vaughan Foundation; funding also was provided by the Daniela Chappard Foundation, Susan and Mac Dunwoody, Fran Magee, Oscar Prato, the Still Water Foundation, Cecilia de Torres, and Natalie Wexler and Jim Feldman.

Funding for the accompanying interactive Web site was provided by a grant from The Edward and Betty Marcus Digital Education Project for Texas Art Museums.

An earlier version of this exhibition and catalogue was produced by the Fundação Bienal de Artes Visuais do Mercosul for the 6ª Bienal do Mercosul, Porto Alegre, Brazil, in 2007 with the sponsorship of Petrobras, Gerdau, and Santander Cultural; material in this catalogue is reproduced with the permission of the Fundação Bienal de Artes Visuais do Mercosul and the authors.

This book is available through D.A.P. / Distributed Art Publishers, Inc.
155 Sixth Avenue, 2nd Floor
New York, NY 10013
Tel: (212) 627–1999 Fax: (212) 627–9484

Library of Congress Control Number: 2009903833
ISBN 978-0-9815738-3-0

Page 1: *Homenaje a Lautréamont* [*Homage to Lautréamont*], 1965 (see p. 20)
Page 2: Francisco Matto in his studio, c. 1966 (see p. 112)

General editor: Gabriel Pérez-Barreiro
Managing editors: Ursula Davila-Villa and Gina McDaniel Tarver
Administrative assistant: Elisa Ferrari
Interns: Doris Bravo and Leslie Moody Castro
Translator (Spanish to English): Jane Brodie
Designer: Zach Hooker
Typesetter and proofreader: Marie Weiler
Color management by iocolor, Seattle
Produced by Marquand Books, Inc., Seattle
    www.marquand.com
Printed and bound in China by C&C Offset Printing Co., Ltd.

ANN WILSON

Francisco Matto: The Modern and the Mythic is the first comprehensive presentation in the United States of the art that this Uruguyan master developed from the 1940s through the 1990s. With more than seventy works on view—including extraordinary wooden sculptures, abstract compositions, intimate portraits, and images of Montevideo, Matto's birthplace—this exhibition exemplifies the Blanton's leadership among institutions presenting, collecting, and producing new scholarship within the Latin American art field. This exhibition continues in the groundbreaking tradition of two of our most successful exhibitions, *El Taller Torres-Garcia* (1992) and *The Geometry of Hope: Latin American Abstract Art from the Patricia Phelps de Cisneros Collection* (2007). A version of *Francisco Matto: The Modern and the Mythic* was originally presented at the 6ª Bienal do Mercosul in 2007 under the curatorial direction of Gabriel Pérez-Barreiro, former Blanton curator of Latin American art and now director of the Colección Patricia Phelps de Cisneros. The version developed for the Blanton Museum introduces to U.S. audiences an artist who, during the 1940s, began developing his own vision of modernity, spirituality, abstraction, and artistic truth.

Francisco Matto was one of the most important students of artist Joaquín Torres-García. With an earnest and early desire to learn, understand, and absorb the legacy of ancient American cultures, Matto joined the Taller Torres-García (Torres-García Workshop, often known as the School of the South), which served as a catalyst for his aesthetic conception. Here he began his pioneering synthesis of pre-Columbian and modern art, forging a new language of abstraction and spirituality.

In addition to this catalogue, redesigned from the Mercosul presentation in an English-language version for the Austin showing, the exhibition is accompanied by an interactive Web publication that incorporates images of his work and video interviews with specialists from different disciplines discussing Matto's most important concerns and interests. The Blanton Museum of Art continues to develop new ways to make our programs and exhibitions accessible to all audiences beyond the museum's walls. Using the Pachyderm multimedia authoring tool, the Blanton exhibition team created this on-line examination of Francisco Matto's work. As the art museum of The University of Texas at Austin, we are especially pleased to be able to involve our exceptional graduate students in researching and interpreting our exhibitions. In this case the interactive Web feature was coordinated by Marya Spont, a graduate student in art education, working in conjunction with the curatorial and education staff of the museum.

This exhibition is only possible thanks to the support and dedication of many people. First of all we must thank Ada Antuña de Matto for agreeing to the exhibition. Oscar Prato, Cecilia de Torres, and Dan Pollock were essential in assisting in research and production at every stage; their tireless efforts are moving testimony to a strong belief in Matto's work. César Paternostro and Robert C. Morgan wrote outstanding texts on a very tight deadline. Our many lenders are to be thanked for their faith and support in the project and generosity in lending the works for their presentation in Austin. Thanks are extended to Annalisa Palmieri and Caroline Dekyndt for their assistance with loaned works for the exhibition. Additionally we thank Carmen Araujo for her design of the exhibition.

We thank Gabriel Pérez-Barreiro for his curatorial expertise in preparing this exhibition for the 6ª Bienal do Mercosul and his support for its presentation at the Blanton Museum of Art. Additionally we thank Ursula Davila-Villa, interim curator of Latin American art at the Blanton, for coordinating every aspect of the exhibition. Ursula worked closely with Steve Bourget, associate professor in the Department of Art and Art History at The University of Texas at Austin, and Jennifer Garner, manager of school and family programs, to conceive and execute a display of ancient South American objects from the art history department's collection to be exhibited alongside *Francisco Matto: The Modern and the*

Mythic. Thanks are extended to the Latin American department who contributed to the project, Gina McDaniel Tarver, curatorial associate, and Elisa Ferrari, curatorial administrative assistant. Additionally, we thank our graduate research interns Doris Bravo, Leslie Moody Castro, and Wendy Earle. The Blanton's education department staff is to be thanked, especially Jennifer Garner and Kristen Fields, former public programs manager, for her tenacity in securing the participation of engaging speakers such as Bettie Sue Flowers, director of the Lyndon Baines Johnson Library and Museum, and Robert C. Morgan, adjunct professor in the Graduate School of Fine Arts at Pratt Institute and catalogue contributor.

The team effort at the Blanton also included exceptional work on the part of the entire staff, in particular Kathleen Brady, director of public relations and marketing; Stacey Cilek, financial manager; Tom Flowers, facility and operations manager; Kurt Heinzelman, interim director of academic and public programs; Sue Ellen Jeffers, registrar; James Swan, technical staff coordinator; and Simone Wicha, director of development; as well as colleagues in their respective departments.

A project such as *Francisco Matto: The Modern and the Mythic* could not be possible without major support from Judy and Charles Tate and the Susan Vaughan Foundation. Funding was also provided by the Daniela Chappard Foundation, Susan and Mac Dunwoody, Fran Magee, Oscar Prato, the Still Water Foundation, Cecilia de Torres, and Natalie Wexler and Jim Feldman. We also thank the Fundação Bienal do Mercosul in Porto Alegre, Brazil, for their assistance in facilitating the presentation of the exhibition at the Blanton Museum of Art as well as the 6ª Bienal do Mercosul sponsors Petrobas, Gerdau, and Santander Cultural. Support for the *Francisco Matto: The Modern and the Mythic* interactive Web site project is provided by a grant from The Edward and Betty Marcus Digital Education Project for Texas Art Museums.

The Blanton is proud to make available to its audiences another distinctive opportunity to explore the rich legacy of Latin American geometric abstraction, one that situates at its core the idea of a modern world rooted in spiritualism, symbolism, and myth.

Introduction

GABRIEL PÉREZ-BARREIRO

An iconic photograph of Francisco Matto shows him leaning against a large U-shaped sculpture atop a hill. His characteristically stern expression and the heroism of his pose are marks of stoicism and romanticism. This vision of a stubborn and committed artist, battling to impose his formal will on the world, provides many clues to Matto's unique artistic personality: a combination of dedication, single-mindedness, deep religious sentiment, and meditative isolation.

Matto's association with the School of the South and the strong impact of his meeting Joaquín Torres-García in 1939 were central to his development as an artist but may also, ironically, have hindered a broader understanding of his work. While Torres-García's teachings and pictorial style were transformative for the history of art, it is also true that not all of his students were able to absorb and process his legacy with equal success. Matto's early exposure to pre-Columbian art and his idiosyncratic early paintings already had established an artistic path for the young artist, so it is likely that Torres-García's influence came to refine and solidify a visual and intellectual temperament that was already largely in place. In Torres-García, Matto found a kindred spirit who shared his fascination with the ancient world and a commitment to abstraction as the highest expression of the human soul. But where Torres-García was mercurial and restless, traveling the globe and taking every possible opportunity to spread the gospel of his artistic philosophy, Matto remained in the same house in the same city for all of his life, rarely engaging with the outside world and shying away from public exposure or commercial success. While many of his colleagues in the Taller Torres-García, most notably Gonzalo Fonseca, José Gurvich, Augusto and Horacio Torres, and Julio Alpuy, followed their master's example and left Uruguay to find new horizons, in Matto's case it seems that isolation and lack of opportunity in Montevideo became positive factors, allowing him to concentrate on his work in an almost monastic setting.

(opposite)
Francisco Matto with his cement sculpture *Forma* [*Form*], 1982, Punta del Este, Uruguay. Photo: Alfredo Testoni.

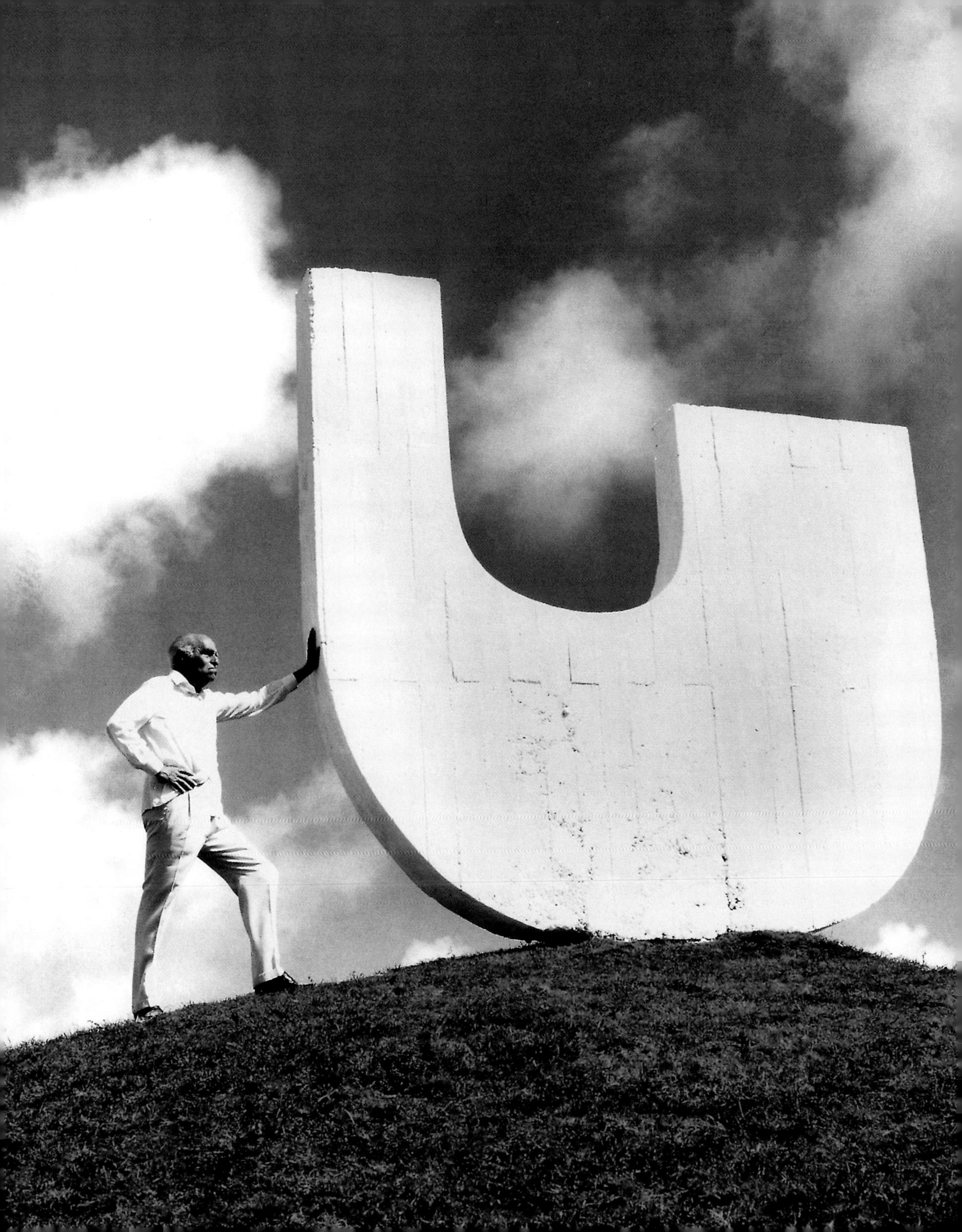

Matto's deeply felt Catholicism also set him apart from his contemporaries, and indeed from most Latin American abstract artists whose Communist orientation precluded religious belief or practice. While most artists of the School of the South were certainly interested in the iconography of the world's religious traditions, their interest was more generic and Platonic, a feeling that pure form was intrinsically and historically connected to spirituality. Matto's early paintings focused on very specific religious iconography, the annunciation or the crucifixion, for example, and throughout his career the word "Dios" (God) would regularly appear embedded in his geometric paintings.

For Matto, art was a form of discipline and access to a universal truth. This rigor is reflected in the limited formal language of his work and its remarkable atemporality. It is almost impossible to date Matto's work on stylistic terms only, as the same motifs and compositions can sometimes appear thirty years apart with relatively little difference in treatment. Matto's work process was circular, focusing on a very limited set of forms that would constantly migrate between drawings, paintings, and sculpture. He reworked small differences with great concentration. This process was anathema to most modern artists, for whom the idea of linear progress was paramount, each new work or series of works effectively superseding and canceling the previous one. Matto's career spanned decades of tumultuous artistic, social, and political change, yet his work was absolutely impermeable, reflecting his steadfast belief in a realm for art that was timeless and absolute.

Of all Torres-García's students, Matto was the most deeply engaged with pre-Columbian art. In fact, he began collecting even before meeting Torres-García in 1939. In the ancient indigenous art of the Americas, Matto found a system that united the geometric with the iconic and spiritual, which is reflected in his preference for Nazca ceramics and Andean textiles. This fusion of structure and symbol was a lifelong pursuit, and photographs of his studio show that he worked with pre-Columbian objects in close proximity, as though they provided him with a constant reminder and inspiration. Matto's substantial collecting of pre-Columbian art led to his creation of a museum in Montevideo dedicated to this purpose. Aside from its historical and cultural importance, the museum also provided a virtual encyclopedia of artistic solutions for Matto. The abandonment of this museum by the City of Montevideo, following its donation to the city by the artist's widow, is one of the great tragedies of Latin American art and denies us the possibility to understand one of the most ambitious projects connecting ancient and contemporary art in the Americas. Matto's relationship with pre-Columbian art is discussed extensively in César Paternosto's essay in this volume. In contrast, Robert C. Morgan presents the work of Matto in dialogue with contemporary trends in painting in the United States, providing a fresh framework in which to discuss his work.

This exhibition was originally organized as part of the 6ª Bienal do Mercosul in Porto Alegre, Brazil. The impulse behind that project was to bring together the major works of this artist for the first time in a comprehensive exhibition, within the framework of an institution that has, for more than a decade, organized many key exhibitions of modern Latin American artists. For this presentation at the Blanton, another pioneering institution in the study of Latin American art, the checklist has been slightly modified and the catalogue revised.

The exhibition and catalogue are structured thematically rather than chronologically. While some subjects do correspond to specific periods, as with the early ports or the late *Caritas*, in most cases the same themes will appear over several decades. The organization of Matto's oeuvre inevitably involves a mixing of categories, so while some works are iconographic (ports, still lifes, *Caritas*), others are related to material and composition (wood reliefs, *Totems*), and others still to a particular type of formal vocabulary that is neither fully abstract nor iconographic, as in the forms or constructions. None of these categories is self-contained, and important relationships exist across categories.

This exhibition provides a rare opportunity to enter into the rich world of a major modern artist whose passionate solitude has kept his work limited to Montevideo and to a small group of fervent admirers elsewhere. It is our sincere hope that many more people will come to appreciate the depth and consistency of Matto's vision for a universal art.

ROBERT C. MORGAN

Francisco Matto is one of the truly extraordinary artists and innovators associated with the studio of Joaquín Torres-García. He is exemplary in many ways: Matto had a superb focus and concentration on the material and philosophical basis of classical form. He had a vital personality capable of inciting new ideas and articulating them through mind and body. He was a man of Earth. In spite of his relatively affluent upbringing in Montevideo, Matto never disowned the intrinsic value of nature. He was humble in acknowledging the influence of others, including his teacher Torres-García and his colleagues at the studio. He was a generous and exuberant artist, willing to share his knowledge of forms with others. Matto exalted in the quiet majestic works of Amerindians and in the sculptural monuments, ceramics, and textiles of his pre-Columbian ancestors. These indigenous sources had an indelible influence on his work. As Cecilia de Torres has made clear, "Matto and his colleagues were sure that they had achieved a unique style: this belief sustained them while they worked far away from the centers of artistic activity, and in a position of marginality respecting them. This conviction and the lack of recognition at the international and the local level strengthened them in their isolation."[1] Relative to this comment, I would like to introduce the work of Matto from the perspective of contrast—namely, to show the cultural infrastructure of the southern hemisphere, specifically of Uruguay, in isolation from that of the New York atmosphere in the sixties. Before proceeding to analyze the work of Matto, it may be helpful to articulate differences between the two cultures, particularly in relation to the artists influenced by Torres-García and the turn toward art commerce in the sixties as exemplified by the U.S. infatuation with Pop art.

The phenomenon of Pop art arrived in the United States in the early sixties, and the implications of its arrival were far more complex than one might have imagined at the time. Artists like Andy Warhol and Tom Wesselmann represented a departure from the interior expressionist impulse in painting and a move toward

1. Cecilia de Torres, "Francisco Matto," in *Francisco Matto: Elemental Forms, 1946–1993* (New York: Galería Ramis Barquet, 2006), 9.

(opposite)
Horacio Torres, *Francisco Matto* (detail), c. 1948. Collection Ada Antuña de Matto, Montevideo.

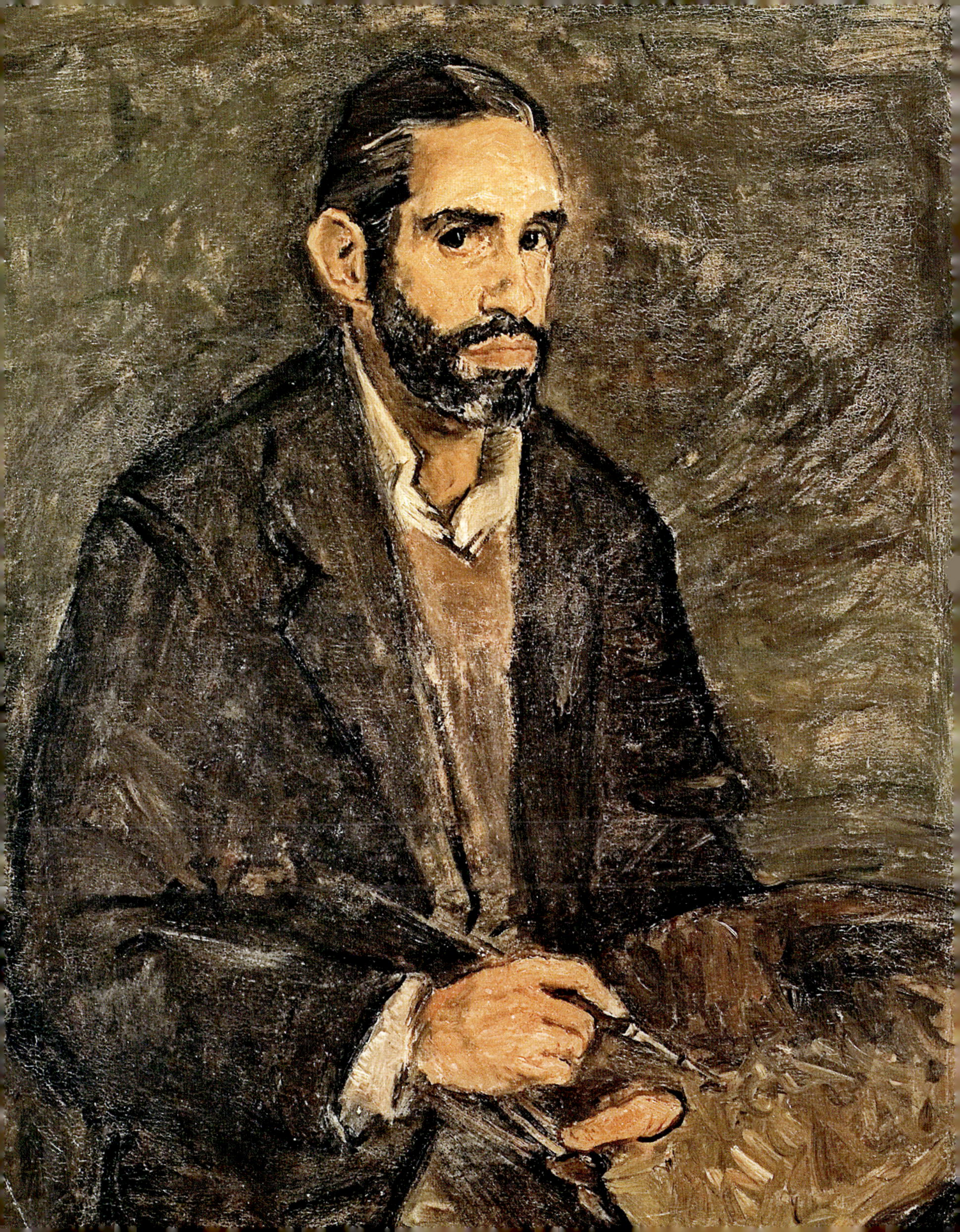

calculations of the external sign. Instead of revealing the plasticity of form, as the work of Joaquín Torres-García and the Constructivists in the School of the South had done, the Pop vernacular was about emblematic power and virtuality. It began the institutionalization of a new anti-aesthetic, which emphasized standardization through the slick surface of logos, labels, and packaging. As an assault on the subtler aspects of form and on the capacity of form to signify spiritual values, Pop art placed emphasis on the commercial sign and its contextual relationships in mass culture. The act of painting was seen as less important than the virtual suspension of the image. By the end of the sixties the subconscious order of signs and the qualitative emphasis on art no longer held a dominant position in U.S. art. It had given way to the signs of commerce.

In contrast the kind of objective vision found in classical form—specifically in the oblique, rugged aesthetic employed by certain artists from the southern hemisphere—was something vastly different from the virtualized images of the north. Artists who began exploring the formal concepts taught by Torres-García in Montevideo during the forties were less concerned with representing the everyday world of commercial signs and logos. Instead they turned their attention to natural forms—basic, organic life-forms—that they converted into geometric signs and symbols that could function within a pictorial or sculptural context. While the artists in the School of the South clearly had their own concerns apart from those of the Abstract Expressionists in New York—more than a decade and a half before Pop art—they did share at this time one idea in common: the search for an abstract vocabulary as a means to express basic human emotions. While artists from the studio of Torres-García may have agreed (or disagreed) on certain issues related to the expressionistic painters in New York, they had no desire to compete. Rather the artists in the south were more interested in a kind of elegance associated with an aesthetic revolution. At least this is how the students of Torres-García—and Matto, in particular—understood their mission and what they hoped to achieve over time.

The force of play is a persistent force in art. In fact play—*homo ludens*—was intrinsic to the spirit of Constructivism and especially to the work of Francisco Matto. As a dedicated member of Torres-García's workshop, Matto was committed to inciting a cultural revolution through a new spiritual perspective on life. The art historian Mari Carmen Ramírez interprets Matto as following the same aesthetic trajectory as Torres-García, a trajectory

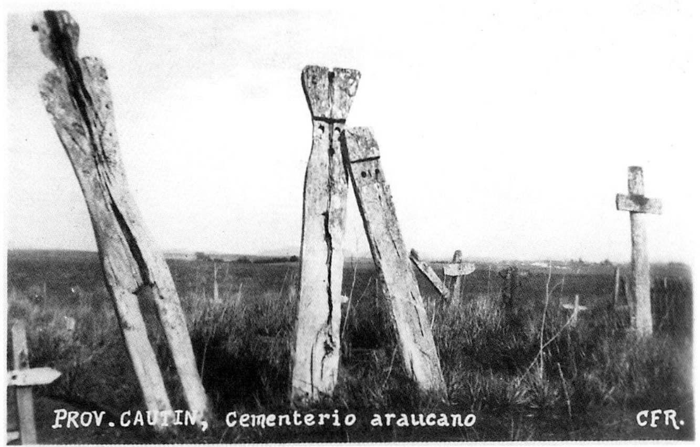

Araucanian Cemetery, Chile. Courtesy Cecilia de Torres, Ltd.

rooted in the belief that "true art consists of the transformation of reality into something else, something metaphysical that is the equivalent of magic."[2] Uruguayan critic Anhelo Hernández saw in Matto's art an objective reality in contrast to a pragmatic approach. Hernández further explained that Matto's work offers "the existence of another world presented principally in tangible terms, without distance, and thus, distant from the world of visuality."[3] There are few artists who can match the grassroots Constructivism of Matto's aesthetic in terms of his understated intellectual prowess and his focus on the genesis of form. Take, for example, the forms found in sculptures such as *Rayo* [*Lightning*] (p. 18) and *Pareja* [*Couple*] (pl. 36). Although nearly twenty years separate the creation of these simple shapes, their directness and reductive pronouncement are apparent—the upright spire in the former and the flattened frontal male and female couplet in the latter. Matto's art moves from the spiritual dimension to a purified form of classical wit. The contrast and commonality between the two sculptures suggest that Matto is a master of mysterious shapes, crude incisions, gritty earth-bound textures, and untamed applications of color. His works appear as the result of a shamanistic impulse, perhaps borrowed from the burial totems used for Indian graves in Chile.[4] Matto saw these rough wooden totems, after passing through the mystical region of Tierra del Fuego, during a voyage by steamer at the age of twenty-one. The memory was somehow stored within the material essence of his deeply evolved aesthetic,

2. Mari Carmen Ramírez, "Re-positioning the South: The Legacy of El Taller Torres-García in Contemporary Latin American Art," in *El Taller Torres-García: The School of the South and Its Legacy*, ed. Mari Carmen Ramírez (Austin: University of Texas Press, 1992), 266.

3. Anhelo Hernández, "Apuntes para un retrato," in *Matto: Pinturas y esculturas* (Montevideo: Imprenta AS, 1991), 13–14.

4. Torres, "Francisco Matto," 8.

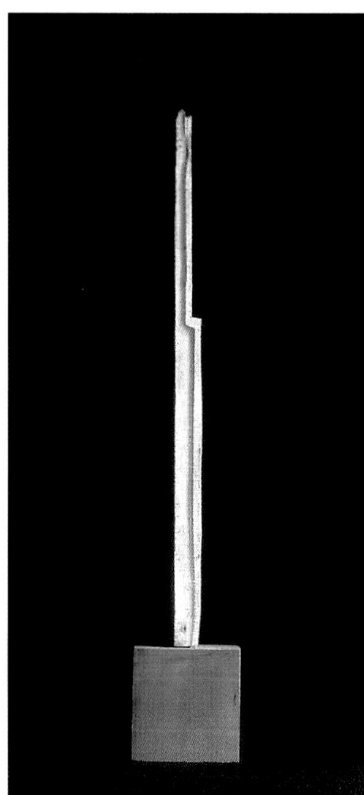

Rayo [Lightning], 1963; oil on wood; 25¼ × 4¼ × 2¼ inches. Collection Galería Oscar Prato, Montevideo.

where he eventually found himself capable of transforming memory and material into a unique spiritual evocation.

To dive into the scope of Matto's "elemental forms" is to marvel at the restraint, the lucidity, the dynamic subtlety, the deep structure, and the sensual, tactile involvement with nature—these are the determining factors that allow us to experience a work of art, a means by which we may grasp the artist's sensibility.[5] This kind of experience is not merely a linguistic one. Nor is it a purely formal exercise. Through direct contact with Matto's work, we may arrive at some subtle, non-discursive avenue of meaning. By attending to the work, our consciousness makes contact with the artist's vision as a distinctive reality, as a higher sensory cognition. Matto's work incites a veritable transformation—another way of seeing. For example the space around his *Totems* may change, as shown in the famous photographs of Carrasco Beach in Montevideo (1983). The spatial referent—the sea, the hillside, or the clouds passing by—enter into the process. Have the forms changed in relation to our perception? Or are they emitting some kind of polarized, telluric light? Although Matto's sculptures are often perceived in a frontal manner, we may read them as having dimensions. We may soon discover that our sense of time has become less fixed, our awareness of temporality more indeterminate. It is conceivable that by allowing such art to cast its spell the viewer may see the sculptures on a different level than expected. Is it possible that such forms can incite a mystical event in time, a fresh look at the world, an intimacy with nature that people who lived thousands of years ago may have understood, allowing them to be within time instead of feeling anxious about the hypothetical present?

During his lifetime Matto opened the threshold of his forms to a new kind of experience: a conjugation of heart, body, and mind. His work recalls the history of all forms, the subjective history of individual consciousness through these forms, and the archaeology of a lived memory. Born and raised in Montevideo—the land of Comte de Lautréamont—Matto never lost faith in himself as an artist. In 1939 he had the fortune to meet Torres-García and shortly after became his student. This changed the direction of Matto's art and life forever. He believed he was in search of "elemental forms," because it was through these forms that he could discover something basic, yet essential, in human consciousness. Matto felt this was the mission of the artist: to come to terms with the real through realizing one's inner nature. While adhering to a Constructivist aesthetic, in the tradition of Torres-García, Matto also had a fundamental belief in nature. For him there was no

5. Cecilia de Torres, *Francisco Matto* (Buenos Aires: Galería Palantina, 1999), 3.

contradiction. Matto loved the barren plains along the Río de la Plata. He thrived on the feeling of nature. This may seem odd for an artist so bent in the direction of geometric construction, but for Matto it made perfect sense.

In one of the photographs taken of the lean-figured Matto standing beside one of the wooden *Totems* installed at Carrasco Beach, he is holding a right-angled section. What this photograph reveals so poignantly is not only the dignity and extraordinary presence of the artist, but the sense that nature is within the human system of thought—that human thought is nature if we allow our thinking process to fuse with our emotions, to connect poetically with who we are as physical, emotional, and intelligent beings in the world. Matto understood this reality as intrinsic to his own sense of self and to his presence as an artist. He wanted to grasp representation as a fact of expression. He had a marvelously delicate way of juxtaposing planar elements—particularly in his later wooden *Totems*—that carried a sensual quality, a grace that lifted the form into a kind of primitive universalism, a kind of raw ether. Matto understood the essential, the symbolic, and the emotional infrastructure that informed space, the elegant maneuvering of space in relation to planar form that can be found in some Amerindian carvings.

Matto compared his *Totems* to a series of roughly carved wooden figures that he saw in Chile in the Atacama desert. While Matto's *Totems* are flatter than those seen in the Mapuche Cemetery in Chile, there is a striking resemblance. There is the basic human necessity to represent. When one sees such affinities, it raises the possibility that the need to inscribe figuration in materials is biological. Much the same can be said about his *Graphisms*. *Graphisms* are paintings, largely composed of grids, in whose many compartments Matto inscribed various signs and symbols. Torres-García developed this formal idea that found a place in the work of many of his students, most notably Héctor Ragni, Rosa Acle, José Gurvich, his sons Horacio Torres and Augusto Torres (in their early work), and, of course, Matto. Coincidently the Abstract Expressionist Adolph Gottlieb had a very similar concept of pictorial structure in his early paintings of the forties.

Matto's *Graphisms* contain a rich variety of shapes and forms—many linear, some cryptic. Shaped, in some instances, like cuneiform marks, these inscriptions tell a story but not a narrative one. They are more about the semiotics of culture as inscribed within memory. For Matto memory was everything, and these signs were the diligent repositories of what he knew to exist below the level

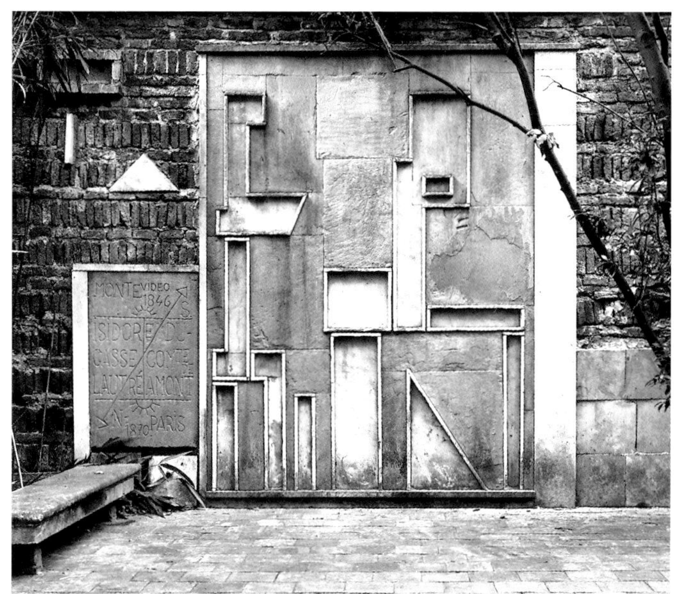

Homenaje a Lautréamont [*Homage to Lautréamont*], 1965; marble and stone; 106 × 90½ inches. Courtesy Cecilia de Torres, Ltd.

of the rational, below the surface of conscious thought. There is a Jungian exegesis somewhere in these paintings, and they are wildly imaginative, purposeful, and subtle. The color is sometimes brooding and dark, sometimes light and effervescent. But there is always the clear knowledge—an alacrity about the method or the process, as the case may be—that these graphics are without dependence on a theoretical proposition outside of what the artist knew and felt at the particular moment when he was painting.

In fact painting and writing begin to touch upon one another in Matto's *Graphisms*. The distinction is not clear. The spirals and the triangles, the pictographic features of the figure (in simplified form), and the emblematic shapes of nature are all combined in a single grid—a marvelous grid, a storyboard, yet without narrative. It is a theater of simultaneous action, a lingering vestige of primal memory that keeps surfacing over and over again. These paintings are so ineluctable, so definitive in their intention, yet so liberated in terms of their execution that the viewer literally becomes carried away, carried into some flight of remembrance, perhaps even below the surface of the unconscious—a point that touches not only upon the collective archetypes of Jung, but on the immanent tactility and formal vocabulary found in pre-Columbian sculpture.

The persistent force of play given to the structure of art is the artist's best recourse to memory, to primordial memory, to getting outside the blockages of everyday conflicts and the discordance of endless banalities. It allowed Matto passage into another world. Matto's world of memory is a special world—a place to gather oneself, to rediscover the sense of self that is so necessary for our spiritual health in a world gone awry with cynicism and calculation. In lieu of commercial imagery and formulas, Matto's revolutionary aesthetic was based on a world of Zen-like play, a world removed from the mirror of the ego. In this sense his art evolved as a clearly conceived vision of his finely tuned heraldic imagination. His classical forms evolved through the course of his life—an incessant journey fueled by simplicity and inspired energy that emerged in the aftermath of despair and occasional doubt. As Matto's formal imagination became increasingly refined, he was impelled to reduce his forms to the more essential terms of meaning. Matto's world was an engagement with non-being, a state of mind that nourishes the fertile soil of enlightenment, as once proclaimed centuries ago by the Chinese sage Lao-tzu.

Francisco Matto
An Artist of the Americas

CÉSAR PATERNOSTO

The only original American creations are those of pre-Columbian art.

OCTAVIO PAZ, *The Labyrinth of Solitude*

In 1932, when he was only twenty-one years old, Francisco Matto took a boat trip along the Argentine coast, going as far as Tierra del Fuego, where he witnessed the lives and customs of the already numbered survivors of certain indigenous groups in Patagonia. He also acquired some baskets from the Onas Indians. This early contact with native cultures, as well as a craving to possess their artifacts, was notably atypical for that generation and for a young man born into the privileged upper bourgeoisie of Montevideo. In the Río de la Plata milieu the norm was to go to Europe to soak up high culture. At the risk of falling into a stereotype, I am referring to the legendary "grand tour" of the rancher tycoons from the region, who traveled with their entire families on slow cruises, often taking along a dairy cow to provide fresh milk for their toddlers. Something similar also was expected in the cultural field—whether the visual arts, music, or literature—where this pilgrimage to the sources was repeated time and again, though of course in much less extravagant circumstances.

We know little of Matto's personal motivations at that young age. Yet, and although the chronology isn't entirely clear, he certainly traveled to the south of Chile as well, going as far as Osorno, the heart of Mapuche territory. There he had the opportunity to see sacred wood carvings or "funeral posts," as those totem-like monuments are called in archeological literature. As I stated above, from the beginning he was driven by a craving to see native cultures in situ and an eagerness to possess their symbolic production. Indeed this was the beginning of a pre-Hispanic art collection that Matto built throughout his life. But, over time, this inclination, this taste, became much more important; indeed, as we shall see, it became a basic motivation behind his artistic work.

In hindsight I don't know whether this fact is relevant when assessing the value of Matto's work. What is certain, however, is that this attitude made him a pioneer in the context of art in the Americas. This ethical, aesthetic attitude helps to recompose what

(opposite)
Francisco Matto with a Paracas tapestry, c. 1958. Courtesy Cecilia de Torres, Ltd.

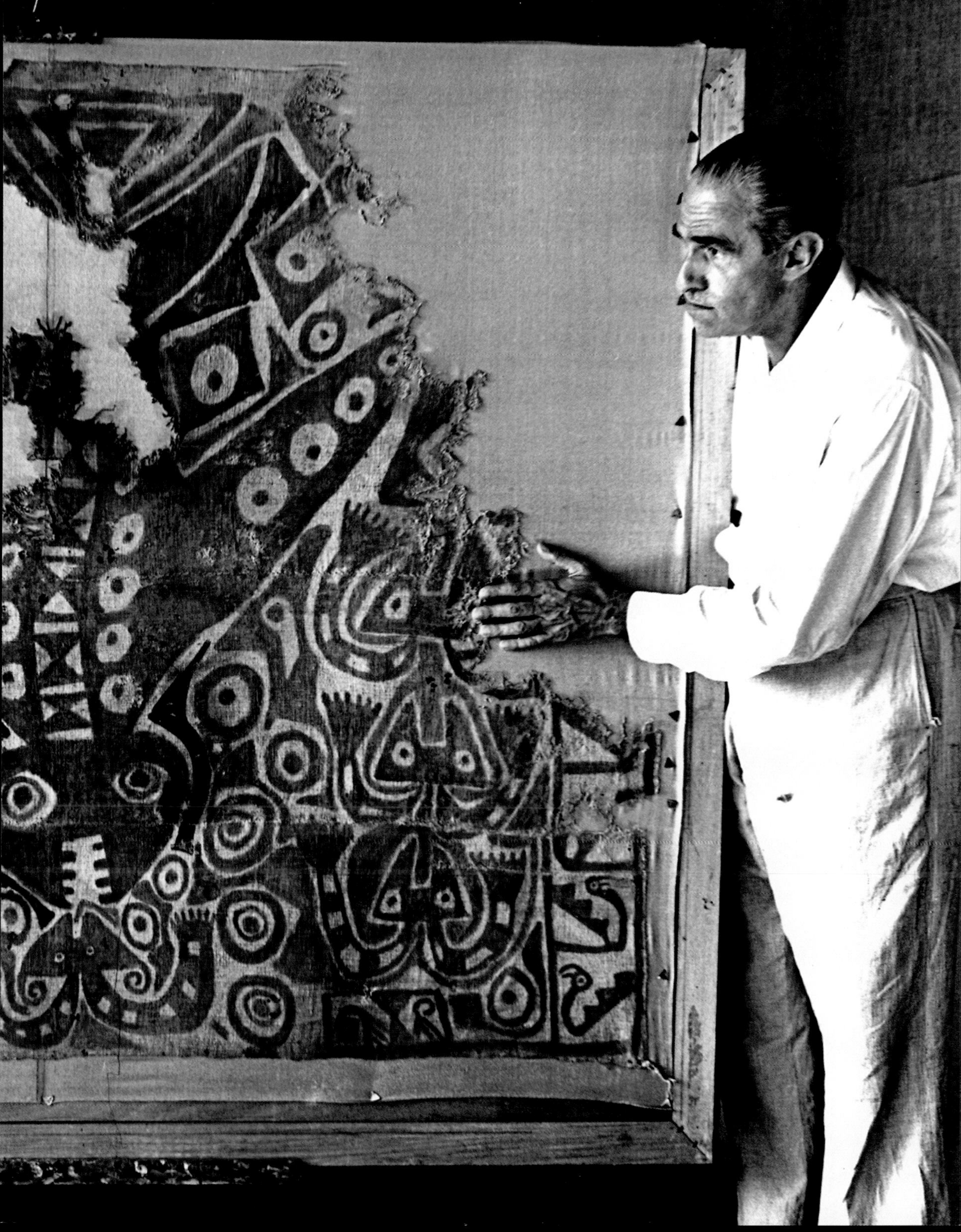

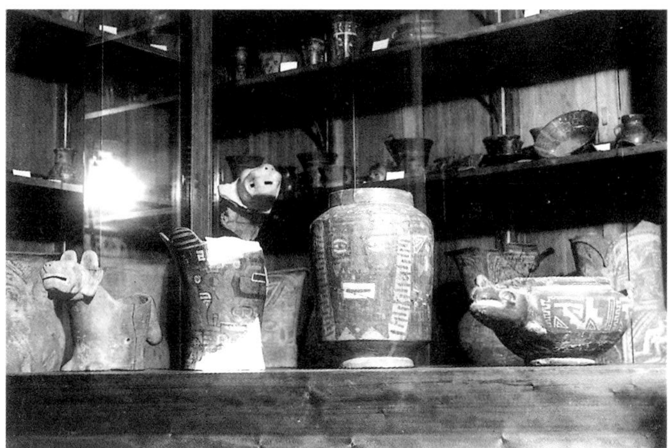

Pieces from Francisco Matto's pre-Columbian art collection in his studio, 1940. Courtesy Cecilia de Torres, Ltd.

I call the cultural equation in Latin American art, considering that the art from our continent has suffered a marked imbalance: an excessive focus and dependence on the—inevitable—European sources (the "Latin-ness") and little or no connection with the only true art from America, which developed before and/or on the margins of European domination.

That early trip to Tierra del Fuego and Matto's contact with a native culture constitute a first and instinctive *shifting of gaze*, a distancing from cultural biases that were almost inevitable for a Latin American. Until the mid-1940s the course of Matto's painting—largely the work of a self-taught artist—was different from that of his collecting. From 1935 to 1945, Matto engaged in diverse pictorial experimentation dependent on European modernism and, especially, the work of Henri Matisse. Yet, and this would take on other meanings over time, Matto later approached the pioneering work of Paul Gauguin, one of the first Western artists to open himself up to the influence of the "other."[1]

In 1939 another decisive event occurred in Matto's life as an artist: he met Joaquín Torres-García and attended his lectures at the AAC (Asociación de Arte Constructivo [Constructive Art Association]), which Torres-García had created in 1935 after returning from Europe.[2] But this happened at the very moment when Torres-García had turned the AAC into a research center for investigating Constructive art and ancient American cultures; this was also the year when Torres-García's definitive text on his interests at

1. See Cecilia de Torres, "El color y la poesía en la obra de Francisco de Matto, 1935–1945," in *Francisco Matto: Poesías y pinturas, 1935–1945* (Montevideo: Galería Oscar Prato, 2003), 36. This is a catalogue for an exhibition that demonstrated the early development of a young Matto who interpreted French modern painting without bias and with total freedom. He experimented with irregularly shaped supports, a striking proposal for still-figurative painting.

2. Later Matto joined the Taller Torres-García, upon its foundation in 1943.

that time, *Metafísica de la prehistoria indoamericana* [*The Metaphysic of Amerindian Pre-History*], was published by the AAC. It is possible to deduce that this encounter served as a catalyst in Matto's aesthetic conception. From then on what was at first a fancy for collecting Amerindian art became a *critical* concern in Matto's work. This new emphasis was thanks to Torres-García's stance in favor of a Constructive art rooted in native sources, which he considered *the* authentic American art.

I believe that Matto's works in wood—which are abstract and sparse—represent his interest in the structure and meaning of art from the Americas more clearly and definitively than do his paintings. As I discuss below I think it is possible to detect a more direct reception of native symbolic production in his works in wood, whereas in his paintings this reception is largely mediated by Torres-García's Constructive Universalism, that is, pictorial construction based on a grid that is regulated by the Golden Section and whose compartments house an array of symbols.

It is important to bear in mind that, until his collection of pre-Columbian art had its own building (the museum opened in 1962), Matto worked amid the pieces in his collection in a sort of "museum-studio." As Cecilia de Torres wrote, "on a timeless and formal plane, these pieces served as a point of reference for his own work."[3] In this sense his *Construcción* [*Construction*], in wood, dated 1947—the first known work by Matto in this material—is strikingly similar to a stylized llama figure in an Andean textile in his collection.

Later, in the seventies, Matto focused on a series of constructions in painted wood: the *Totems*. In addition to the abiding vision of Mapuche carvings—a decisive influence that gives these pieces the definition I spoke of above—in these works we can discern the convergence of other influences, for example, an Incan ritual scepter in his collection.[4] *Máscara* [*Mask*] (pl. 47), from 1979, also contains many references; though *Idea*, a wooden piece by Torres-García dated 1942, might have been its most immediate model, this piece brings together not only Amerindian traditions but also tribal arts from Africa and Oceania. *Venus* (pl. 47) is a reference to classical Greece; and *Tablas de la ley* [*Tablet of the Law*] (1979) alludes to the Old Testament tradition. And, of course, in the title of the work *Hombre universal* [*Universal Man*] (pl. 49), from the same *Totems* series, one can see the influence of Torres-García's universalist teachings.[5]

There is another work in wood, c. 1979, in the shape of a guitar whose front is marked by sets of parallel lines in a certain

3. See Cecilia de Torres, "Pilgrimage to the Sources of Amerindian Art," in *Abstraction: The Amerindian Paradigm* (Brussels: Société des Expositions du Palais des Beaux-Arts de Bruxelles, 2001). This catalogue accompanied a show that I curated that opened at the Palais des Beaux-Arts in Brussels (May 2001) and then traveled to IVAM in Valencia, Spain (October 2001).

4. As observed by Mari Carmen Ramírez in "Repositioning the South: The Legacy of the Taller Torres-García in Contemporary Latin American Art," in *El Taller Torres-García: The School of the South and its Legacy*, ed. Mari Carmen Ramírez (Austin: University of Texas Press, 1992).

5. It's worth recalling that, in addition to the aforementioned piece *Idea*, during those years Torres-García also made works in painted wood, some with titles that make specific reference to Amerindian culture such as *Pachamama*, from 1944, and *Padre Inti*, also from 1944. *Monumento* [*Monument*], c. 1943, in unpainted wood, can also be seen within this context; one of its blocks—which are reminiscent of Inca constructions—has a solar image (*Inti*) carved into it.

reference to the lines painted on a Mapuche ritual drum, the shaman's *kultrun*. Similarly I would like to point out a striking parallel with another pioneer in abstraction. In *Kandinsky and Old Russia: The Artist as Ethnographer and Shaman*, Peg Weiss suggests that Kandinsky was basically inspired by the simple figures and marks on the drums of Lapp shamans, which represented diagrams of the universe and cosmic forces.[6] Grounding her argument on the ethnographic expeditions that Kandinsky undertook in the Vologda region in 1889, Weiss maintains that Kandinsky's perceptions of the shamanic sense of vernacular art in that region at that time were decisive to his later development. This is, of course, a very narrow interpretation, and one that I cannot share because it disregards all the other sources that supported Kandinsky as he moved toward abstraction, such as Theosophy, his knowledge of mysticism, and Zen Buddhism. Nevertheless this reference helps to make clear an important point: that through searches that are parallel, though removed significantly in time and geography, these two pioneers of modern abstraction (which Matto was in the context of art in the Americas) encountered an otherness that served as a crucial catalyst. In other words, although it is far from evident in the dominant discourse, I believe that a geometrically structured abstract art is not only informed by but, indeed, largely anticipated by non-European modalities. Or, in any case, modalities from non-European cultures and from ancient Europe.

I think it is possible to verify a reading different from the linear and formalist view of Western painting that goes from Manet to abstraction, a reading that, as we know, was set up by the Eurocentric Greenbergian discourse. I am speaking of a phenomenon that has been virtually ignored. Though one could speak of the *intersection* or *reception of the other*, geometric abstraction as *the irruption of the other* is, in any case, a phenomenon that entails crossovers; it approaches from the sidelines, altering the linearity of the figurative pictorial tradition, that is, of mainstream Western painting. Because even if we accept that abstraction is a deliberate development of the Cubist grid (Mondrian, Malevich), how can we separate out the reception of tribal African sculpture that

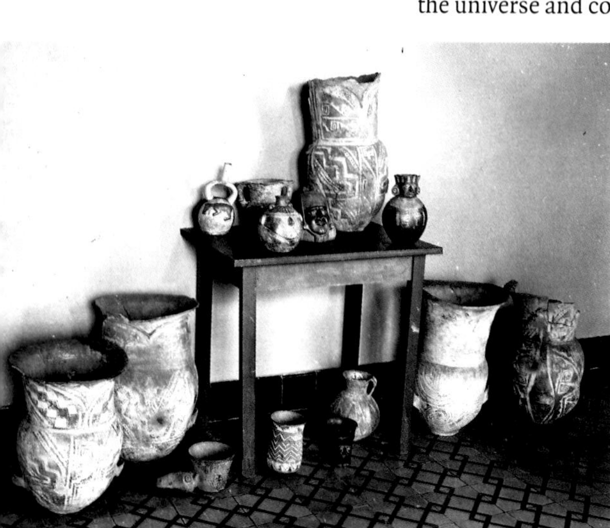

Pieces from Francisco Matto's pre-Columbian art collection in his studio, 1940. Courtesy Cecilia de Torres, Ltd.

6. Peg Weiss, *Kandinsky and Old Russia: The Artist as Ethnographer and Shaman* (New Haven and London: Yale University Press, 1995).

takes place at the origin of Cubism, modern abstraction's natural forefather? The distinguished Brazilian theorist Mário Pedrosa pointed out this question to me more than thirty years ago, in a memorable encounter in Santiago de Chile, in 1971, when Pedrosa and Aldo Pellegrini were cultural advisors to the Allende administration. Though that position appealed to me at the time, I didn't see it as clearly as I do now. More recently John Golding has supported this view with the observation that "both Mondrian and Malevich had already reached Abstraction through their immersion in Cubism which, in turn, had found in tribal art one of its two greatest sources of inspiration."[7]

When I speak about the irruption of the *other*, I am thinking of geometrical shapes in art that evolved outside of Western civilization, art that existed long before the modern version with which we are familiar and that appeared late in the global history of art. To understand this we must, if possible, try to counter the formidable power of the hierarchical "art/ornament" discourse. This dichotomy is what has made it impossible to perceive that what is called "ornament" is really the central art of non-European cultures and of the pre-modern West.[8]

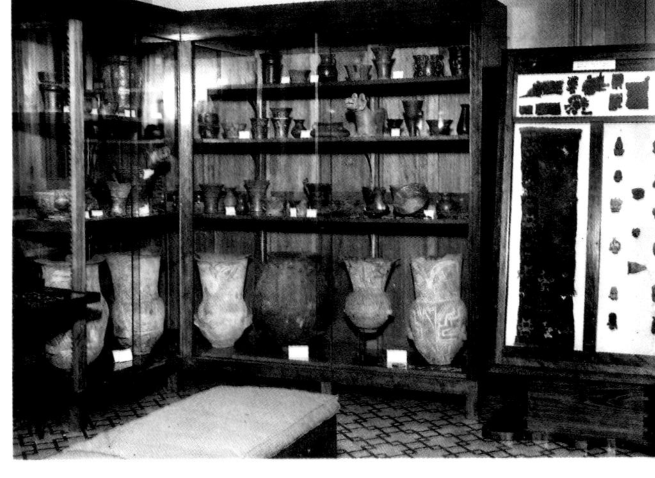

Pieces from Francisco Matto's pre-Columbian art collection in his studio, 1940. Courtesy Cecilia de Torres, Ltd.

At the very heart of those archaic abstract shapes, we find an eminent conceptual model, if not its material presence outright: I am speaking of the textile grid (which obviously includes its forefather, basketry). It is not difficult to verify that long before the emergence of the Eurocentric "fine arts" model, centered on representative easel painting, weaving was unquestionably significant in the production of flat, geometrical artistic shapes. There are numerous and varied examples of this, such as geometrical symbols that have been in use for thousands of years, from the Neolithic period to the Bronze Age. Other more recent examples exist in Africa. I am thinking of the sub-angular geometries in the paintings by Mbuti women from the Ituri Forest in northeastern Congo and the raffia weavings of the Kuba and Berber tapestries. The quadrangular conception of the tantric *yantra* recalls prehistoric geometrical schemes derived from textile structures. And, of course, there are also the paradigmatic geometrical shapes

7. John Golding, *Paths to the Absolute: Mondrian, Malevich, Kandinsky, Pollock, Newman, Rothko and Still* (Princeton: Princeton University Press, 2000).

8. This is the basic argument of my essay "Abstraction: The Amerindian Paradigm," in the catalogue of the same name; see n. 3.

produced by the weaving grid in the marvelous Andean tradition. Furthermore there is another strain of geometric art foreign to Western culture, one that results from Islamic culture's sophisticated knowledge of mathematics and geometry. I am speaking of the intricate tile and mosaic compositions of Islamic mosques and palaces that only occasionally make use of the eight-point star that originates in the textile grid. Mistakenly the West has always seen these as ornamental.

In the Americas the physical presence of the *other* is inevitable. There are, on the one hand, the impressive ruins of what are called the pre-Hispanic "high cultures" of the past and, on the other, the reality of still-surviving native cultures. Yet to be succinct—I cannot discuss the complex issue of the ambiguous relationship between the peoples of the Americas and the pre-European past—many outstanding examples of Amerindian art still are displayed in anthropology or natural science museums, like some sort of epistemological hybrid: scientific specimens, certainly, but with *another* sort of beauty, an aesthetic that has left the Western canon aside. In fact since the end of the nineteenth century, scientific paradigms—anthropology, ethnography, archeology—have placed certain boundaries between modern art and native symbolic production, boundaries that, generally speaking, only artists are able to cross.[9]

In fact it is in the vision of artists that the *instant recognition of the art* within the artifact occurs. And, more specifically from my point of view, what is for the scientist or typical art historian merely a mute or chance "geometrical decoration" on a textile or clay vessel becomes, for the artist, a formative experience, a "lesson in abstraction." Of course I am thinking of those artists whose work has given rise to this perception, this exchange, and, it must be added, they are not exactly a majority—which attests to the ambivalent relationship with pre-Columbian art I describe above.

Francisco Matto is one of the first of such artists. His first contact with native cultures took place in the thirties, though then he was still as a very young collector. That was the decade when his mentor Torres-García, Anni and Josef Albers in Mexico, and Adolph Gottlieb in Arizona began to work on this intersection of artistic sources. And if Matto's first works in connection to the native arts of the Americas came later, in the forties, they are, in a sense, contemporaries of Gottlieb's later production—his *Pictographs* series from the forties and fifties—and of Barnett Newman's theoretical and curatorial work.

9. It is interesting to remember that in 1946, Barnett Newman organized a show of paintings by Indians from the Pacific Northwest at Betty Parsons gallery in New York. Some of the pieces in that show came from the Museum of Natural History. Along these lines Edmund Carpenter astutely observed that by moving these pieces from one place in the city to another, the curators of the show "declassified them as scientific specimens and reclassified them as art." Cited by James Clifford in *The Predicament of Culture: Twentieth Century Ethnography, Literature and Art* (Cambridge, Mass.: Harvard University Press, 1988), 239.

Two still-unpublished texts grew out of Matto's focus on art from the Andean world. The first, *Variantes formales y decorativas de las cerámicas de Tiahuanaco* [*Formal and Decorative Variants in Tiahuanaco Ceramics*], Matto wrote in 1946. The second, an untitled text, he probably wrote around 1950; it also refers to Tiahuanco art as "seen by a contemporary artist."[10] In these texts Matto analyzes some of the works in his own collection and repeatedly mentions the direct and orthogonal nature of this iconography: "The purity of a style where horizontal and vertical lines take precedence over curves." This means, in other words, the decisive influence of the textile—the grid pattern—on the iconography of Andean art. That is what I have called, on other occasions, a "tectonic abstraction," a concept that implies both the paradigmatic orthogonality of the textile structure and the constructive techniques.[11]

Matto first visited Europe in 1950 and, in an interview with Carlos Cipriani López, said, "I went [to Europe] for the first time in the fifties and, by that time, I no longer liked European art. To be quite frank, there was nothing, no movement that I was interested in."[12] Cecilia de Torres, citing Pierre Loeb, stated that "after the war, the moment had come for others to invade the European consciousness," in reference to Wifredo Lam, another artist whose work intersects with the ancestral cultures of his native Cuba.[13] She added, "the work of Matto after 1945 represents a plausible course for the North and South American artist, the *others*; instead of continuing modern movements from Europe, working from them, merging them with Amerindian culture."[14]

10. Matto's writings are now in the archives of the Getty Research Institute, Los Angeles.

11. For further information on this subject, see chapters 7 and 8 of my book *The Stone and the Thread* (Austin: University of Texas Press, 1996), as well as my aforementioned essay in the catalogue *Abstraction: The Amerindian Paradigm*; see nn. 3 and 8.

12. "Con Francisco Matto: Las fuentes de lo mágico," *El País*, Montevideo, Year IV.

13. In *L'aventure de Pierre Loeb. La Galerie Pierre, Paris, 1924–1964* (Paris: Musée d'art moderne de la ville de Paris,1979).

14. Torres, "El color y la poesía," 36.

Ports

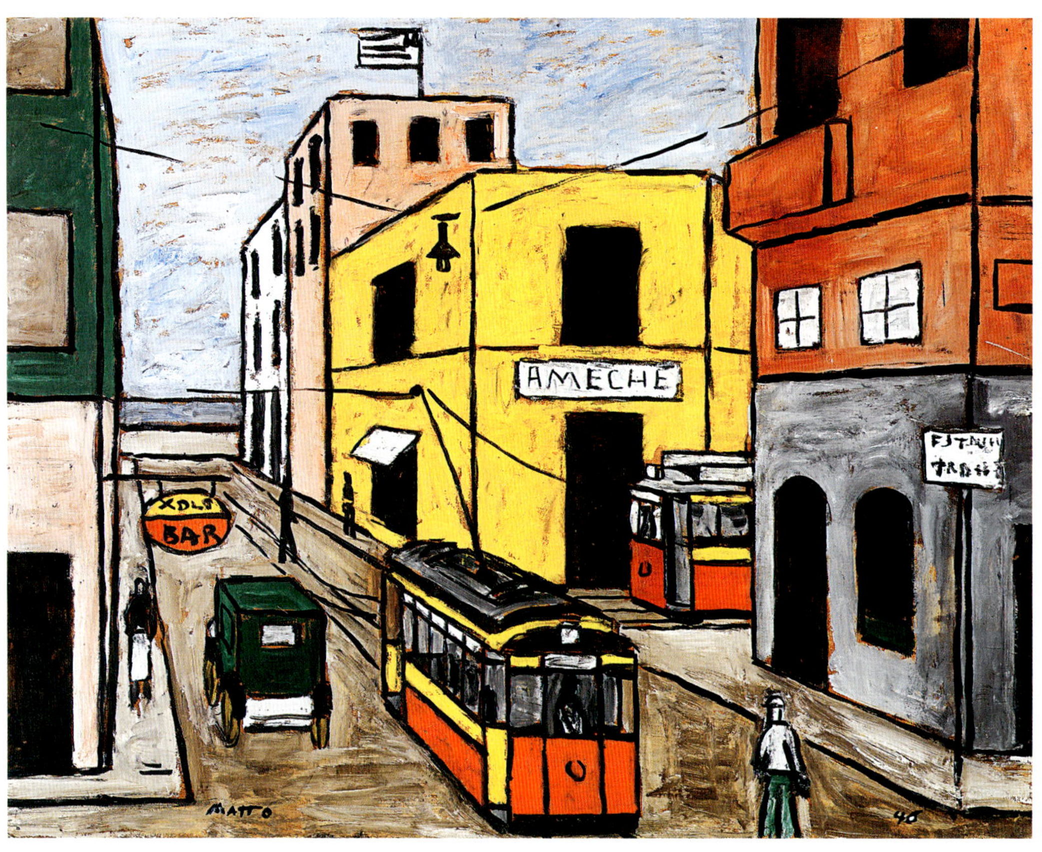

AMECHE
XDLS
BAR
MATTO

1 Perspectiva Ciudad Vieja [Perspective of Ciudad Vieja] 1946;
oil on cardboard on canvas; 31½ × 41¼ inches. Private collection.
Photo: Hugo Maertens.

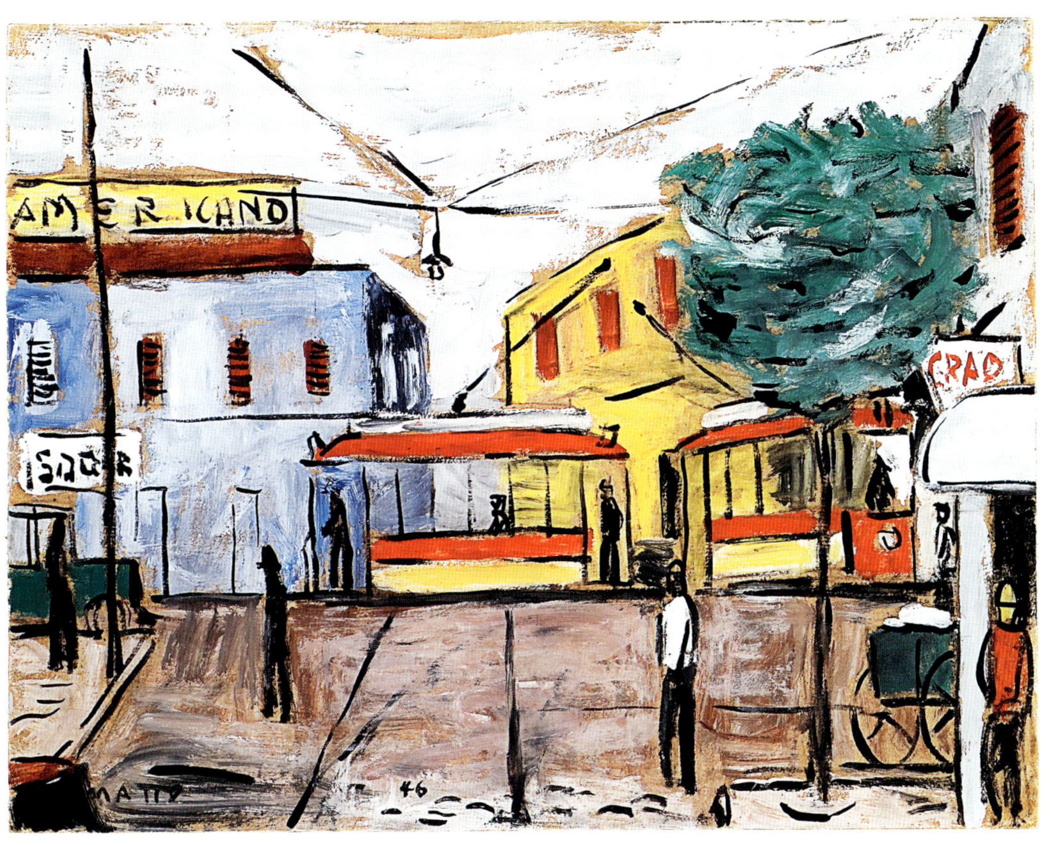

AMERICANO
SOR
CRAD

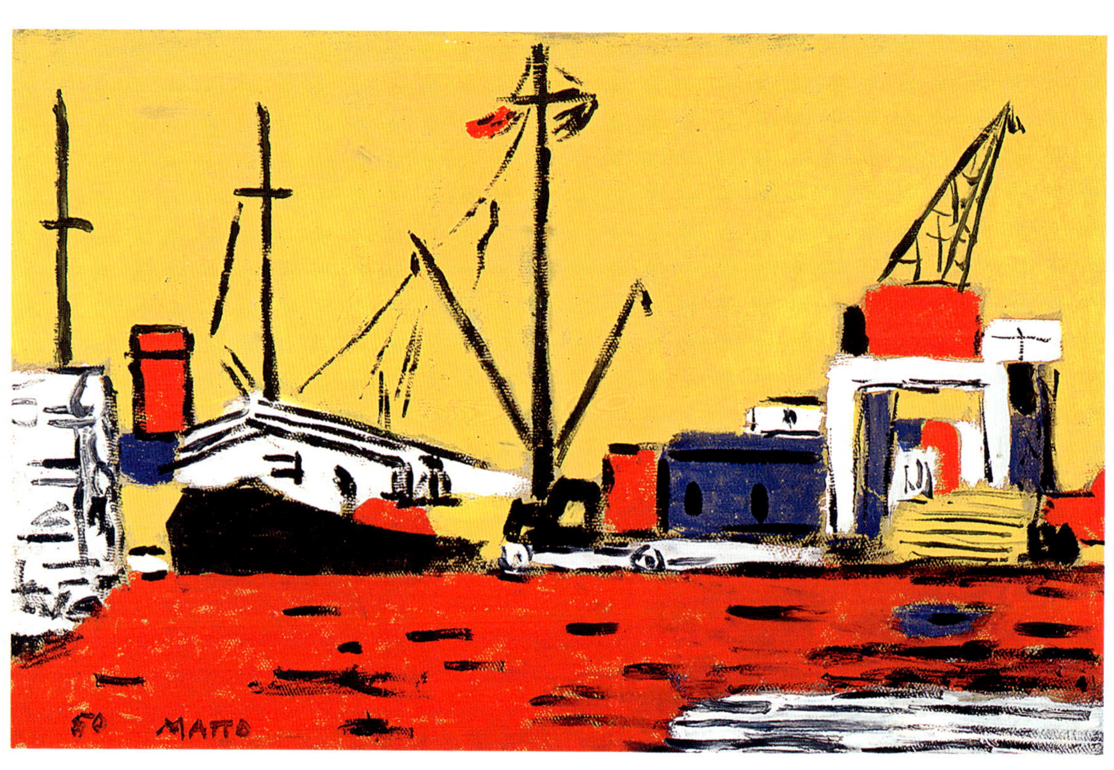

3 Puerto en colores primarios [Port in Primary Colors] 1950; oil on cardboard; 20¾ × 31½ inches. Collection Daniela Chappard Foundation. Photo: Arturo Sánchez.

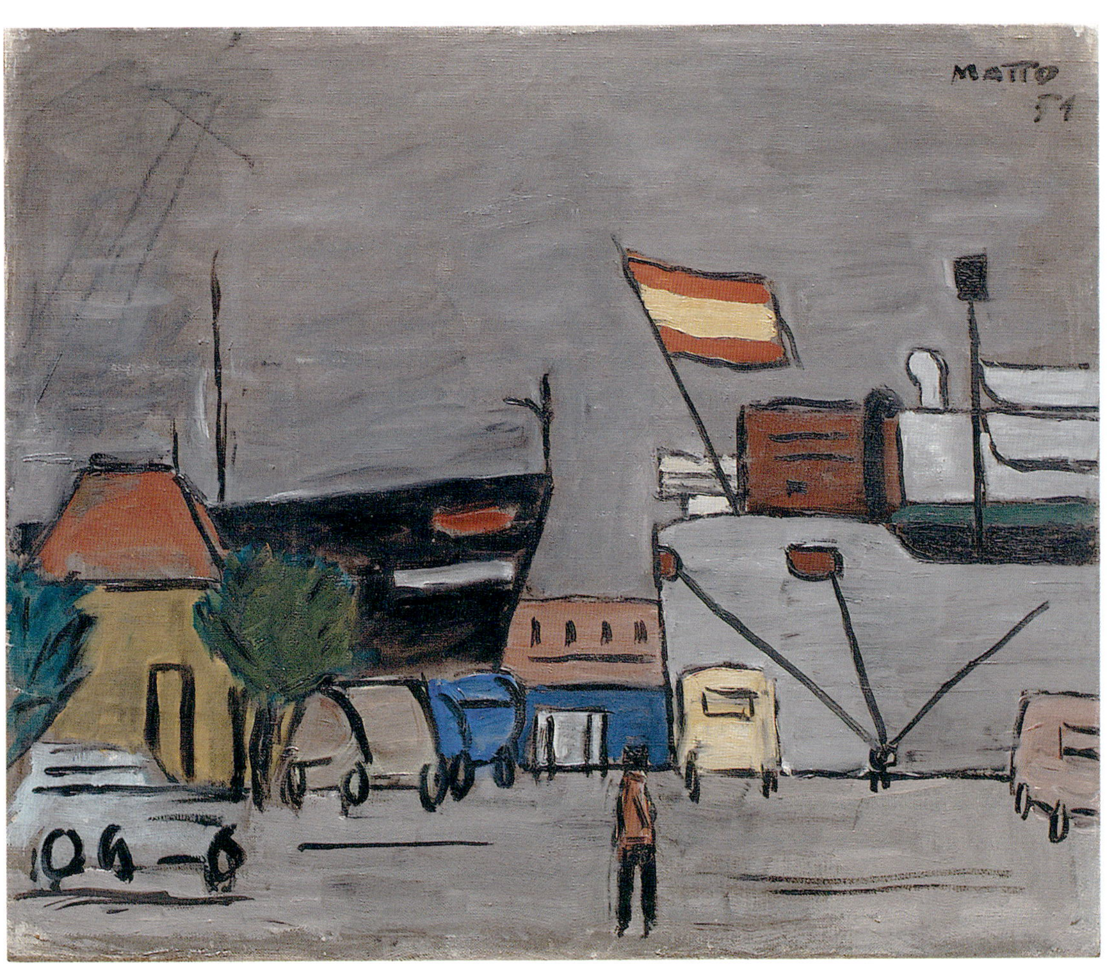

4   Paisaje del Puerto [Port Landscape]   1951; oil on canvas;
19¾ × 23⅝ inches. Collection Galería Oscar Prato, Montevideo.
Photo: Galería Oscar Prato.

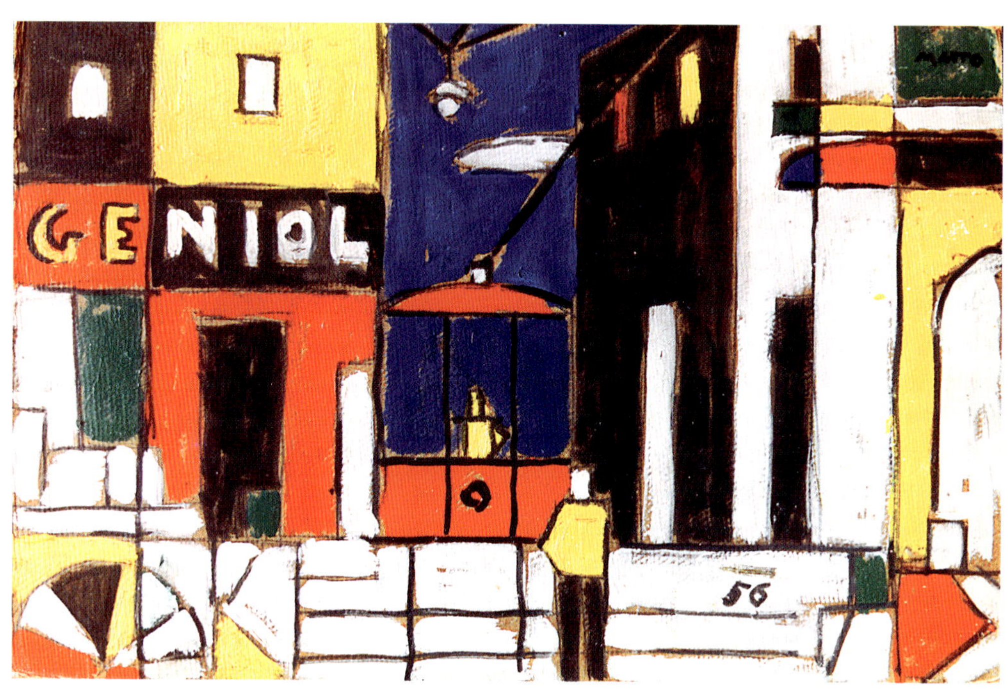

5   Geniol 1956; oil on cardboard; 12¼ × 18¾ inches. Collection Estate
of the Artist, Courtesy of Cecilia de Torres, Ltd. Photo: Arturo Sánchez.

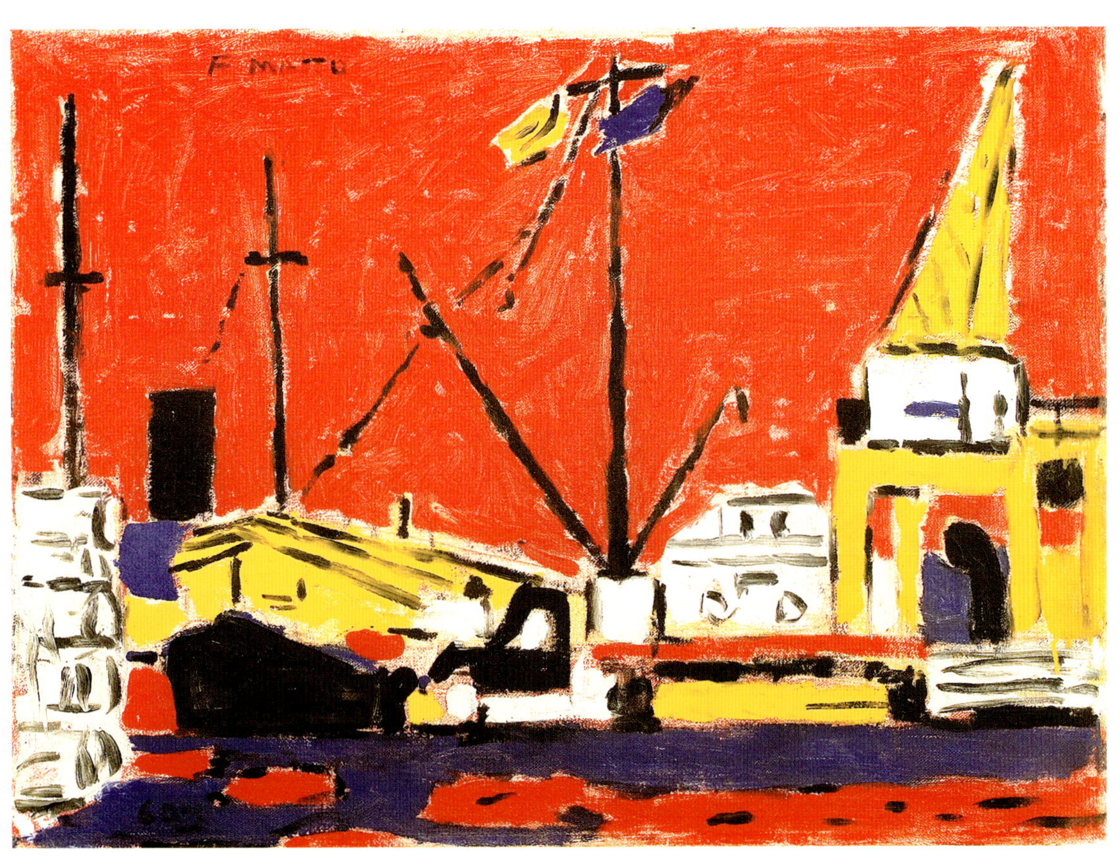

6 Puerto con cielo rojo [Port with Red Sky] 1960; oil on canvas; 19¾ × 27⅝ inches. Collection Estate of the Artist, Courtesy of Cecilia de Torres, Ltd. Photo: Arturo Sánchez.

Still Lifes

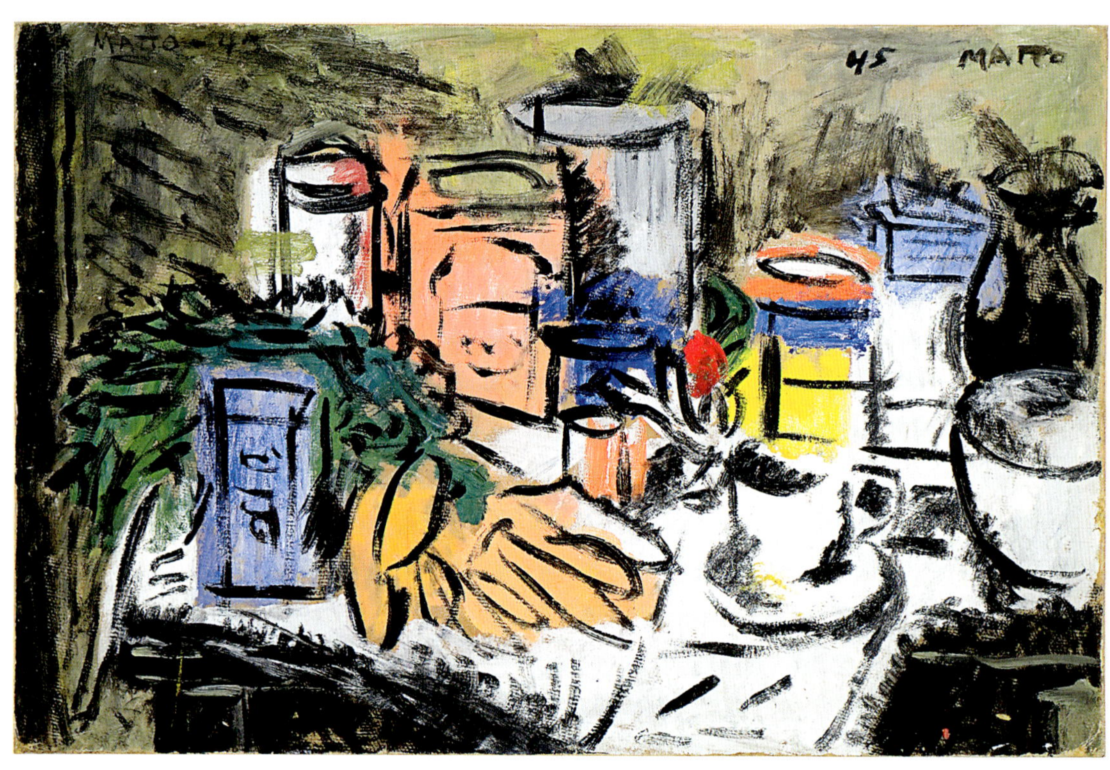

7 Naturaleza muerta [Still Life] 1945; oil on cardboard on canvas;
21 3/4 × 33 3/8 inches. Collection Judy and Charles Tate, Houston.
Photo: Fábio Del Re – Vivafoto.

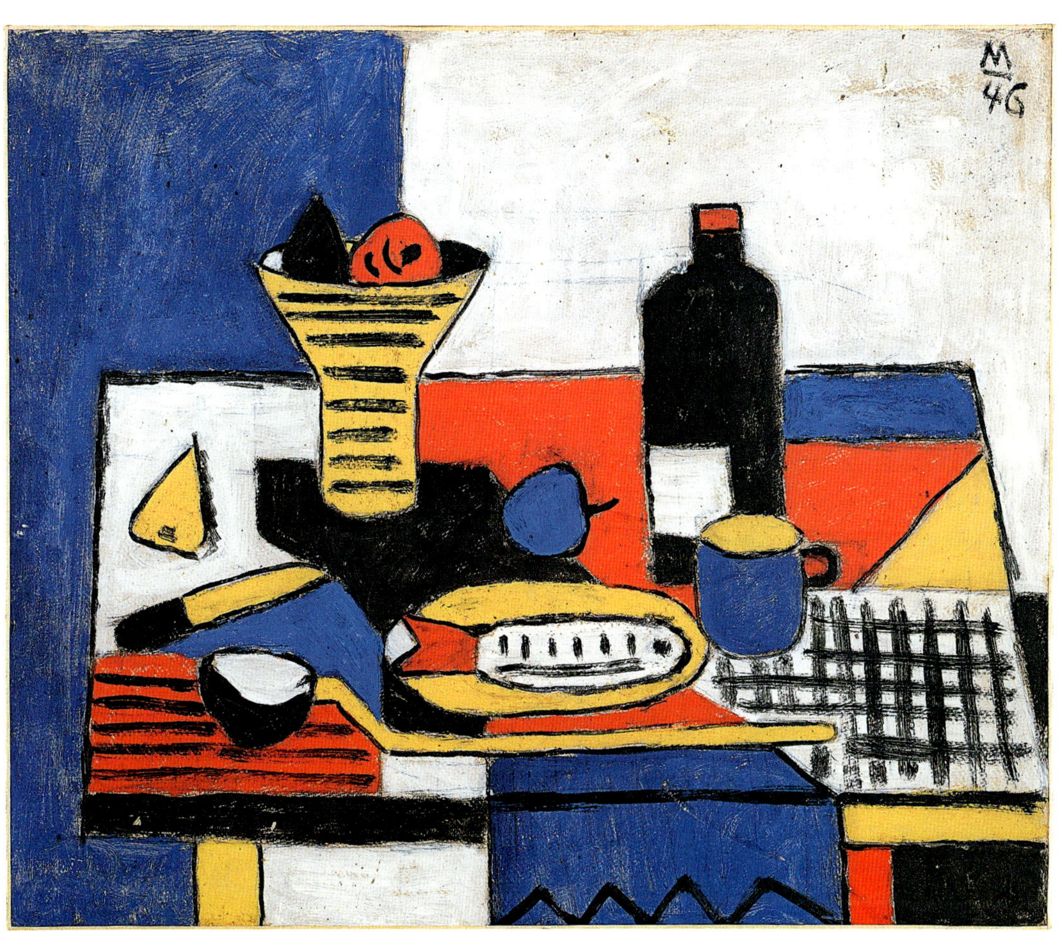

8   Pintura constructiva [Constructive Painting] 1946; oil on cardboard; 20½ × 24¼ inches. Collection Estate of the Artist, Courtesy of Cecilia de Torres, Ltd. Photo: Larry Lamay.

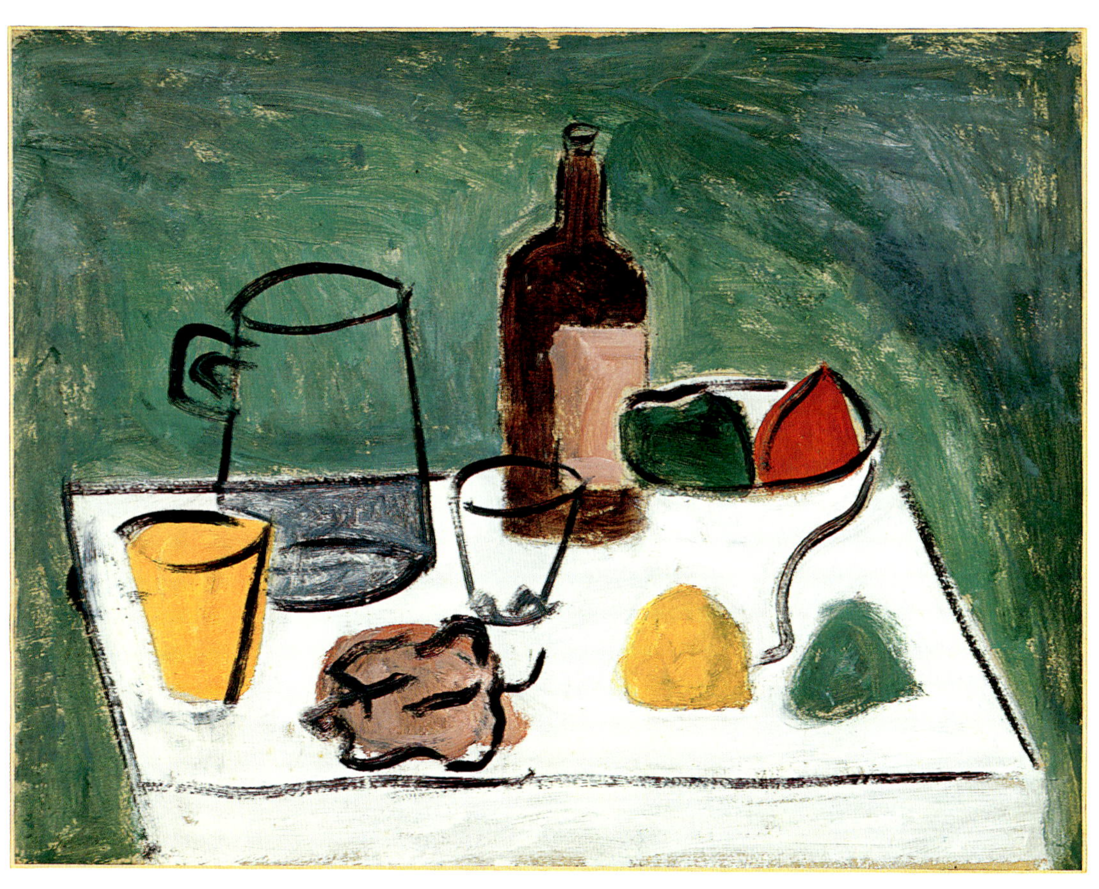

 Naturaleza muerta con plano de color y línea [Still Life with Color Plane and Line] c. 1947; oil on cardboard; 19½ × 25⅞ inches. Collection Estate of the Artist, Courtesy of Cecilia de Torres, Ltd. Photo: Larry Lamay.

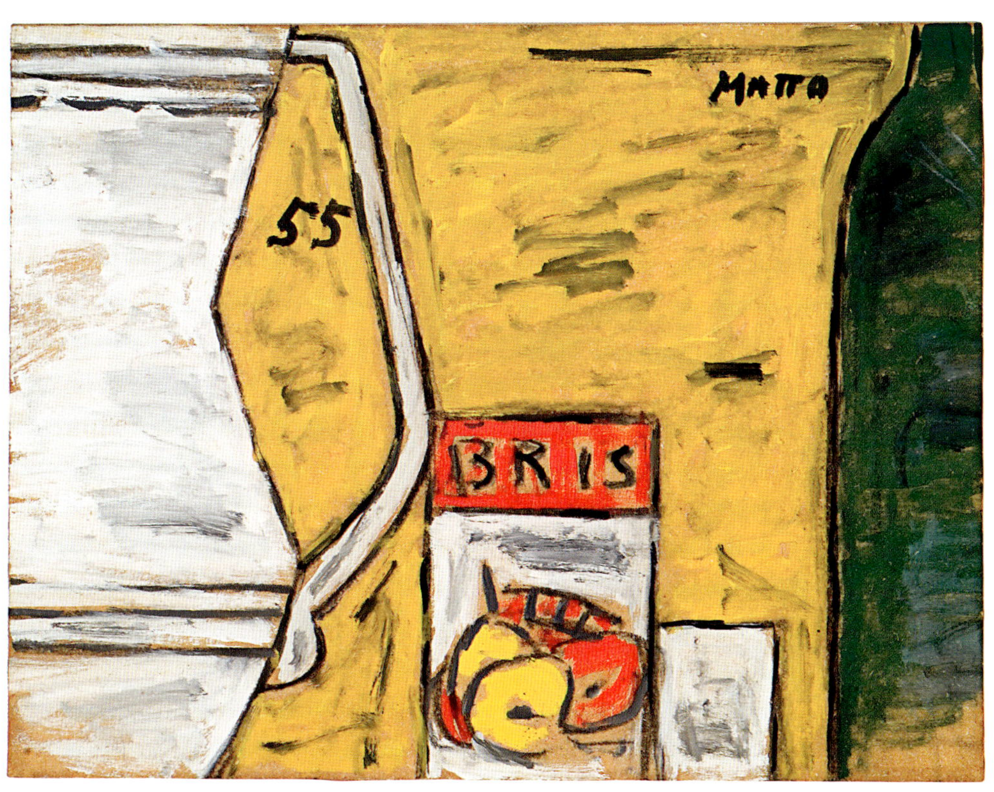

10   Naturaleza muerta con jarra [Still Life with Jar] 1955; oil on cardboard; 12⅝ × 16½ inches. Collection Ada Antuña de Matto, Montevideo. Photo: Fábio Del Re – Vivafoto.

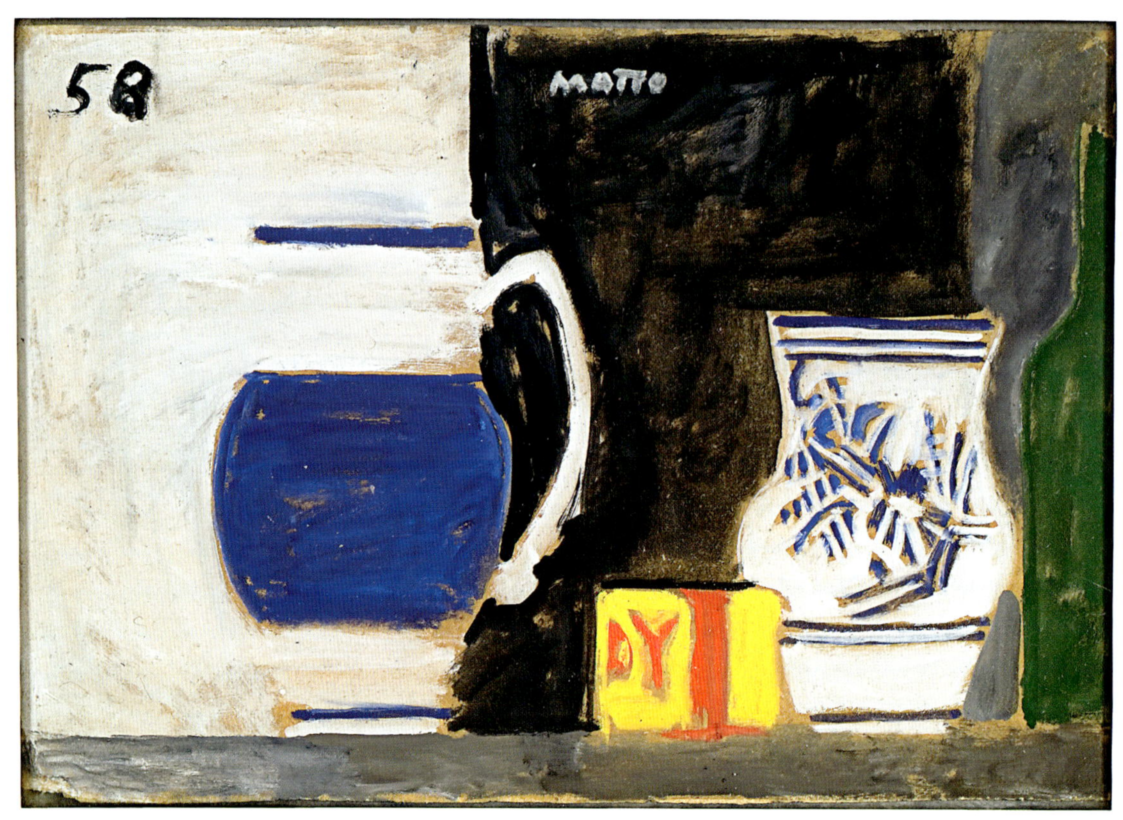

11   Naturaleza muerta [Still Life] 1958; oil on cardboard; 13 × 18⅛ inches.
Private collection. Photo: Fábio Del Re – Vivafoto.

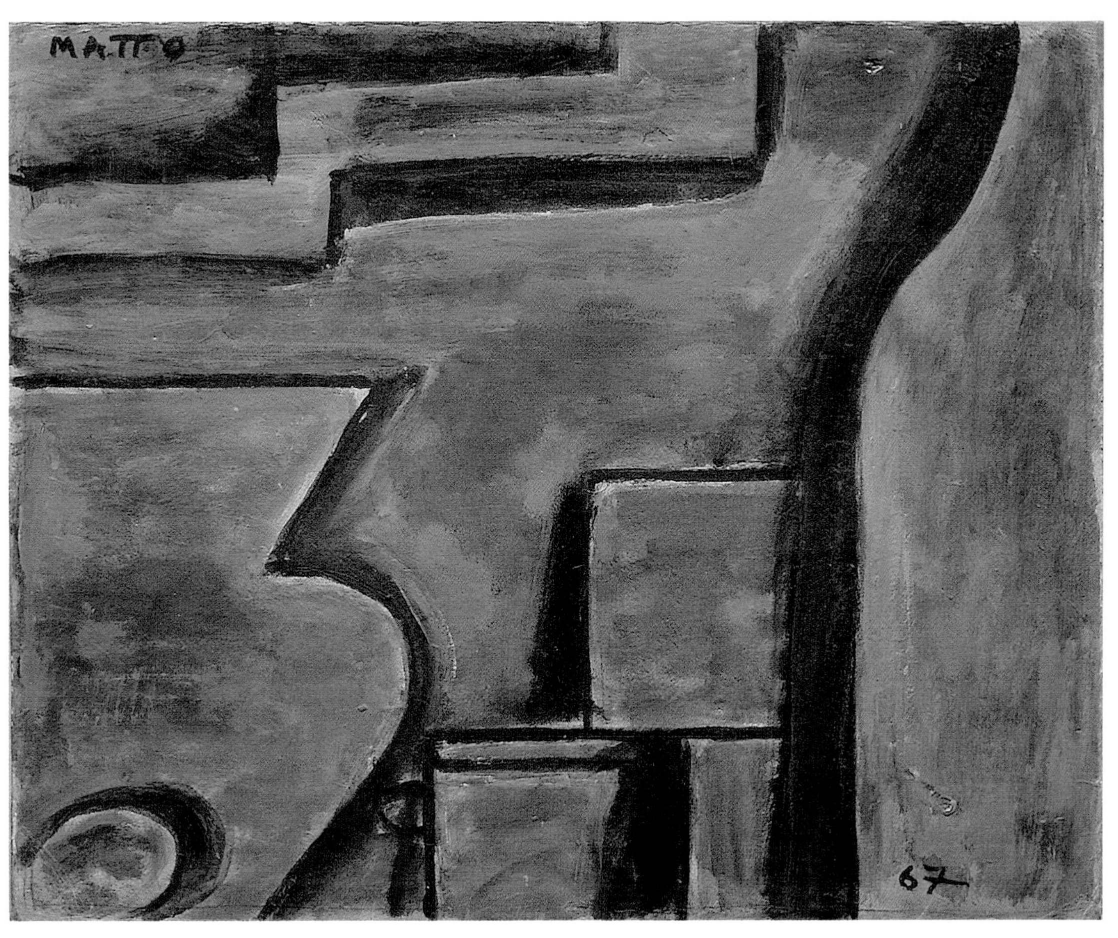

12   Naturaleza planista con botella y jarra [Planar Still Life with Bottle
and Jar] 1967; oil on cardboard on canvas; 16¾ × 22 inches. Collection
Galería Oscar Prato, Montevideo. Photo: Galería Oscar Prato.

Constructions

13 salome 1950; oil on cardboard; 18⅛ × 24⅜ inches. Collection Estate of the Artist, Courtesy of Cecilia de Torres, Ltd. Photo: Arturo Sánchez.

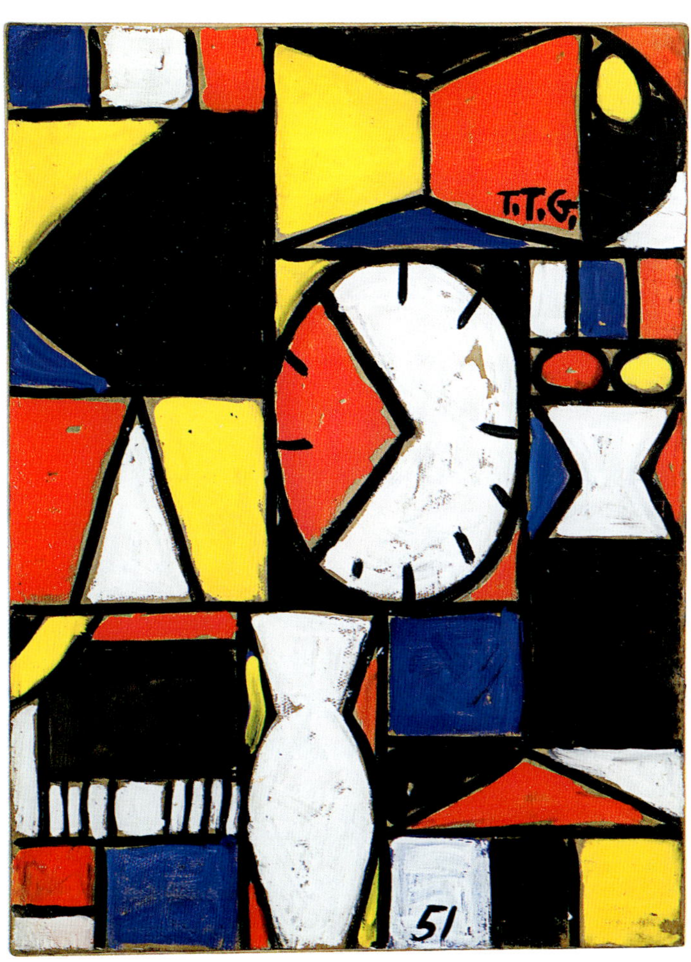

14   Constructivo con reloj [Constructive with Clock] 1951; oil on cardboard on canvas; 26⅝ × 19⅞ inches. Collection Galería Oscar Prato, Montevideo. Photo: Fábio Del Re – Vivafoto.

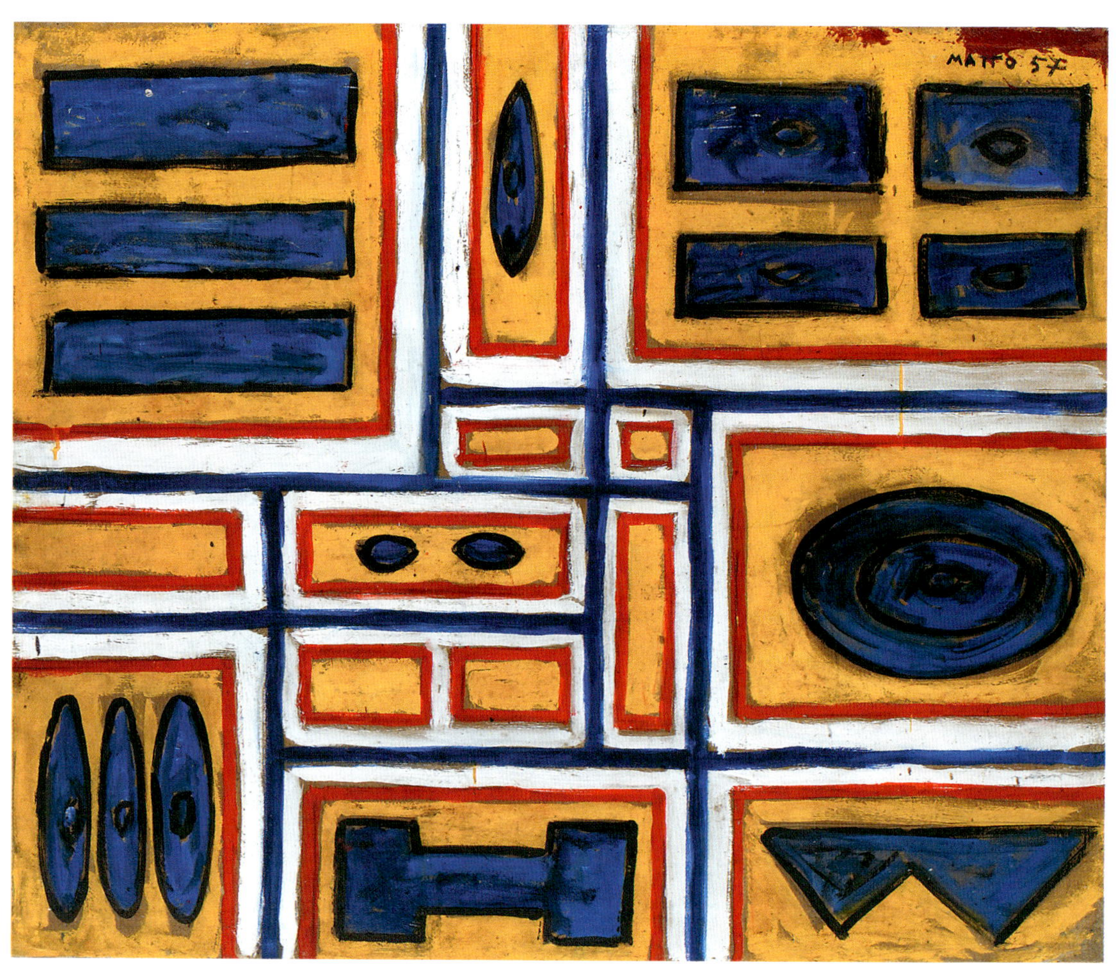

MAFO 57

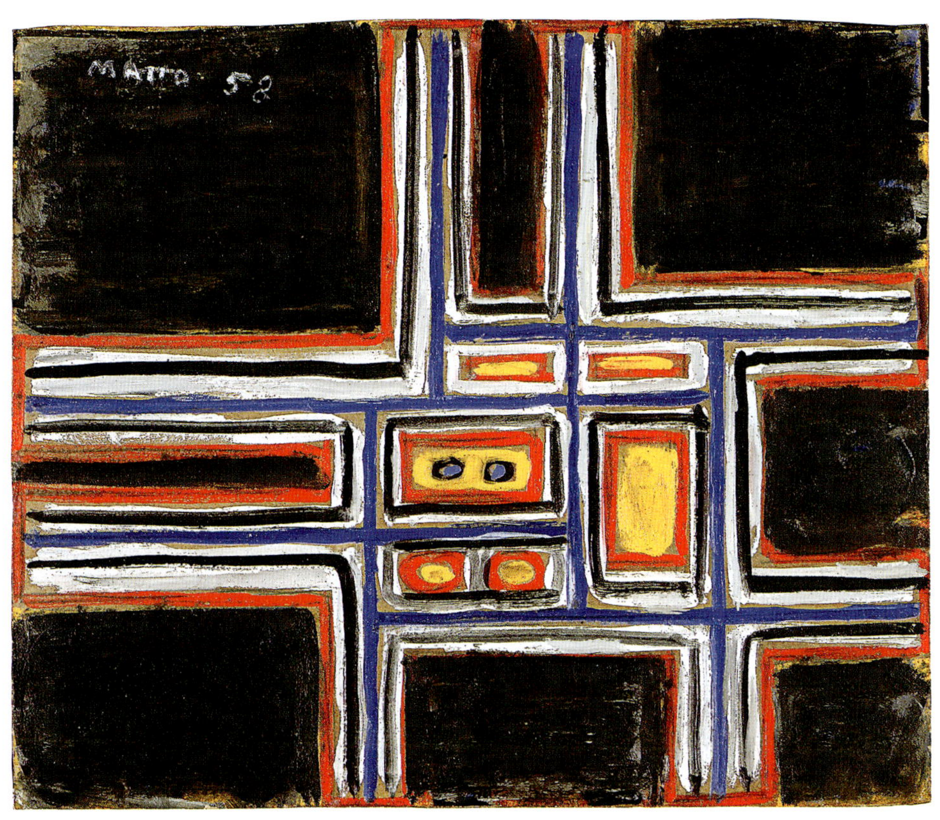

16   Composición sobre fondo negro [Composition on Black Background] 1958; oil on cardboard; 15 × 18 inches. Collection Blanton Museum of Art, The University of Texas at Austin, Gift of Judy and Charles Tate, 2004.172. Photo: Rick Hall.

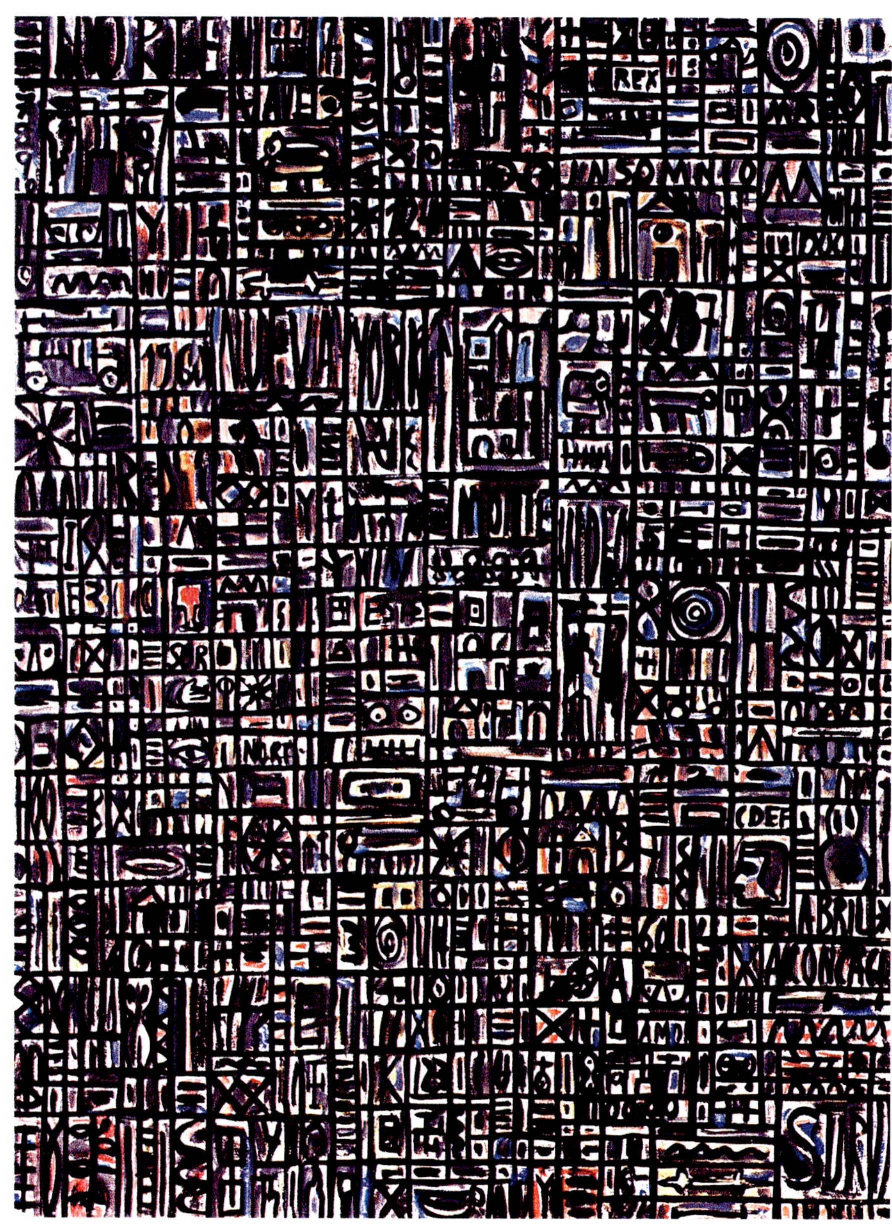

17 Constructivo Nueva York [Constructive New York] 1960; oil on cardboard; 40⅞ × 31¼ inches. Collection Estate of the Artist, Courtesy of Cecilia de Torres, Ltd. Photo: Arturo Sánchez.

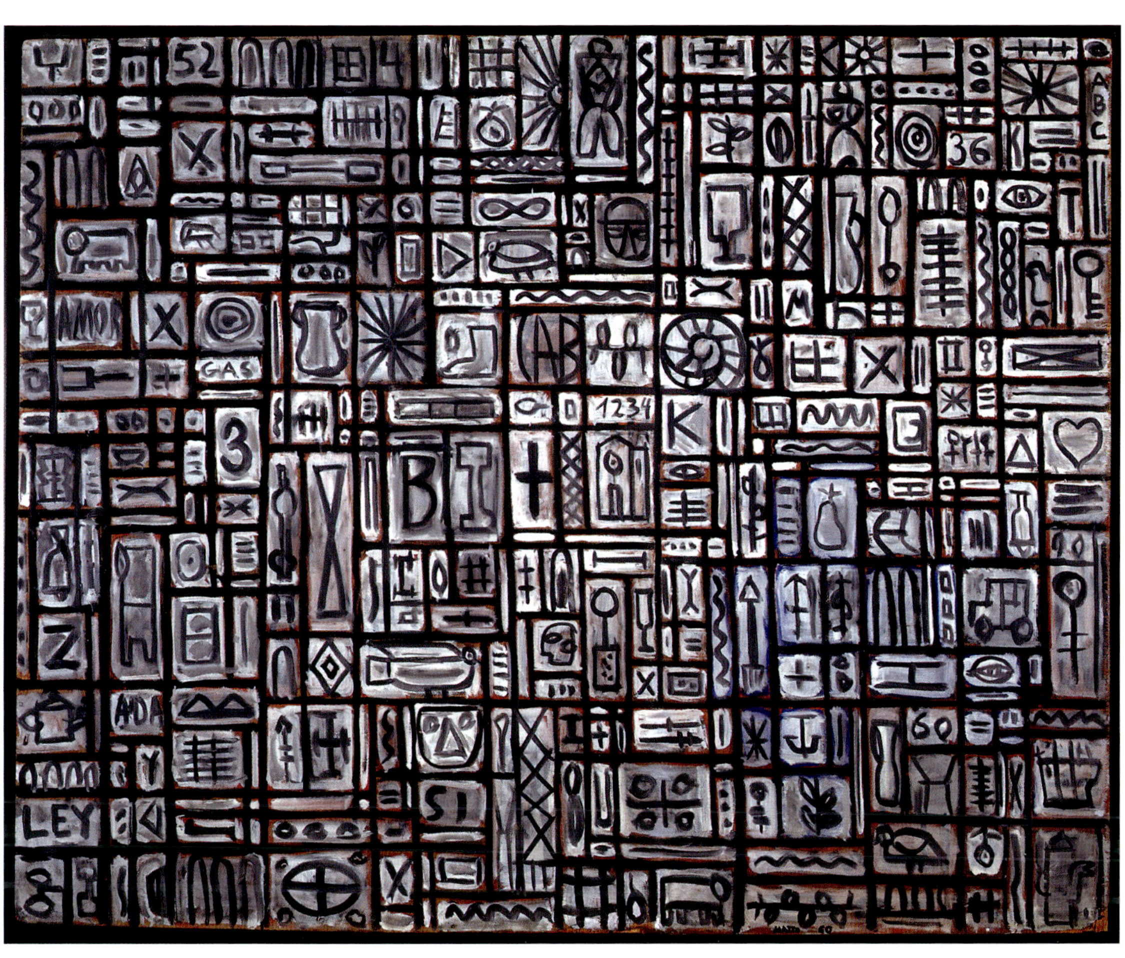

18 Retícula blanco y negro [Big Black and White Grid] 1960; oil on wood; 55 × 70½ inches. Collection Estate of the Artist, Courtesy of Cecilia de Torres, Ltd. Photo: Arturo Sánchez.

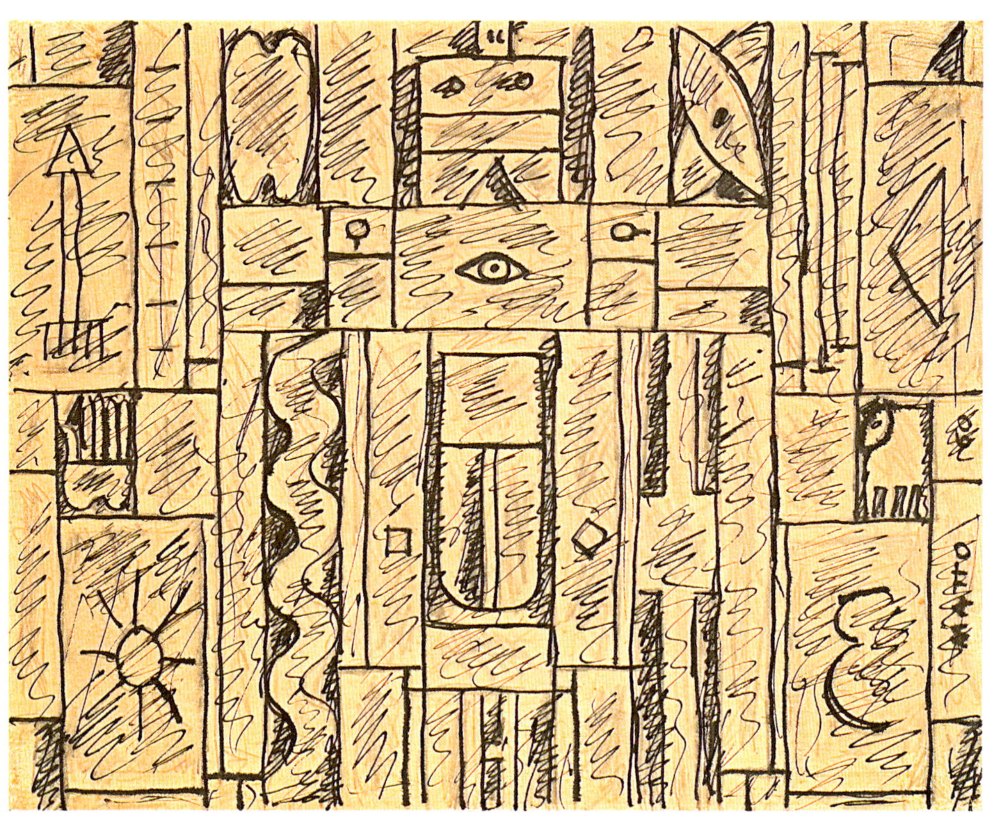

19 Constructivo sin color [Colorless Constructive] 1962; ink and pencil on paper; 8½ × 11 inches. Collection Estate of the Artist, Courtesy of Cecilia de Torres, Ltd. Photo: Arturo Sánchez.

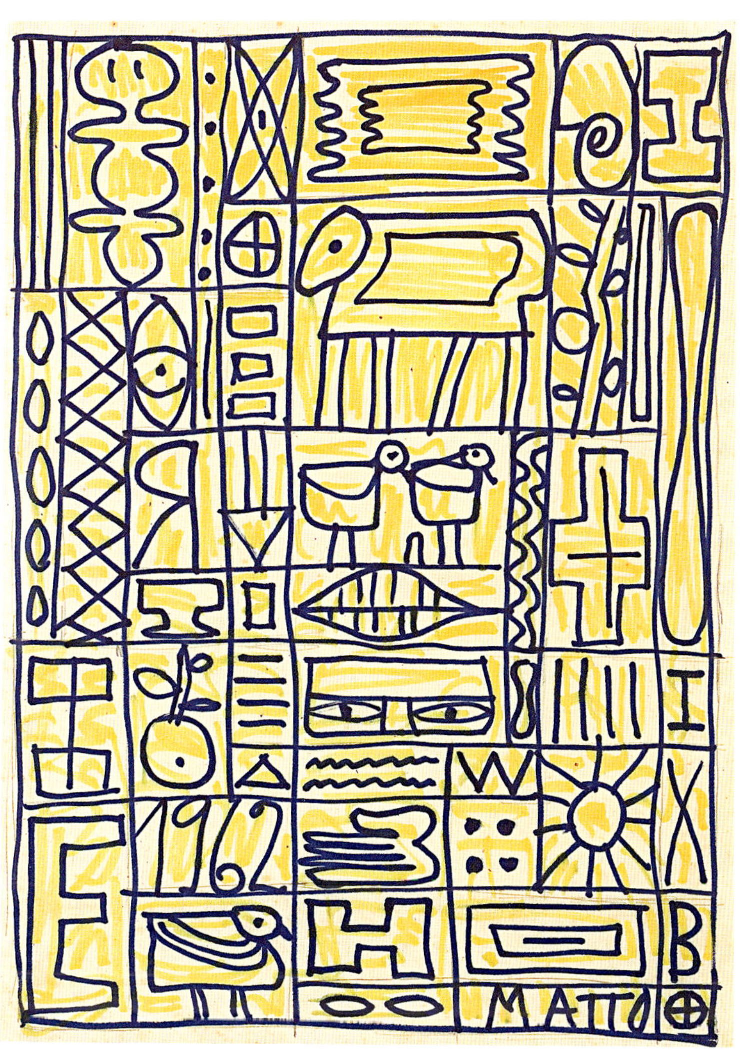

20   Rejilla en amarillo y azul [Grid in Yellow and Blue] 1962;
Magic marker on paper; 15 × 11 inches. Collection Estate of the
Artist, Courtesy of Cecilia de Torres, Ltd. Photo: Arturo Sánchez.

21 Construcción en cinco colores [Construction in Five Colors] 1963; oil and graphite on cloth; 43¾ × 25⅜ inches. Collection Judy and Charles Tate, Houston. Photo: Fábio Del Re – Vivafoto.

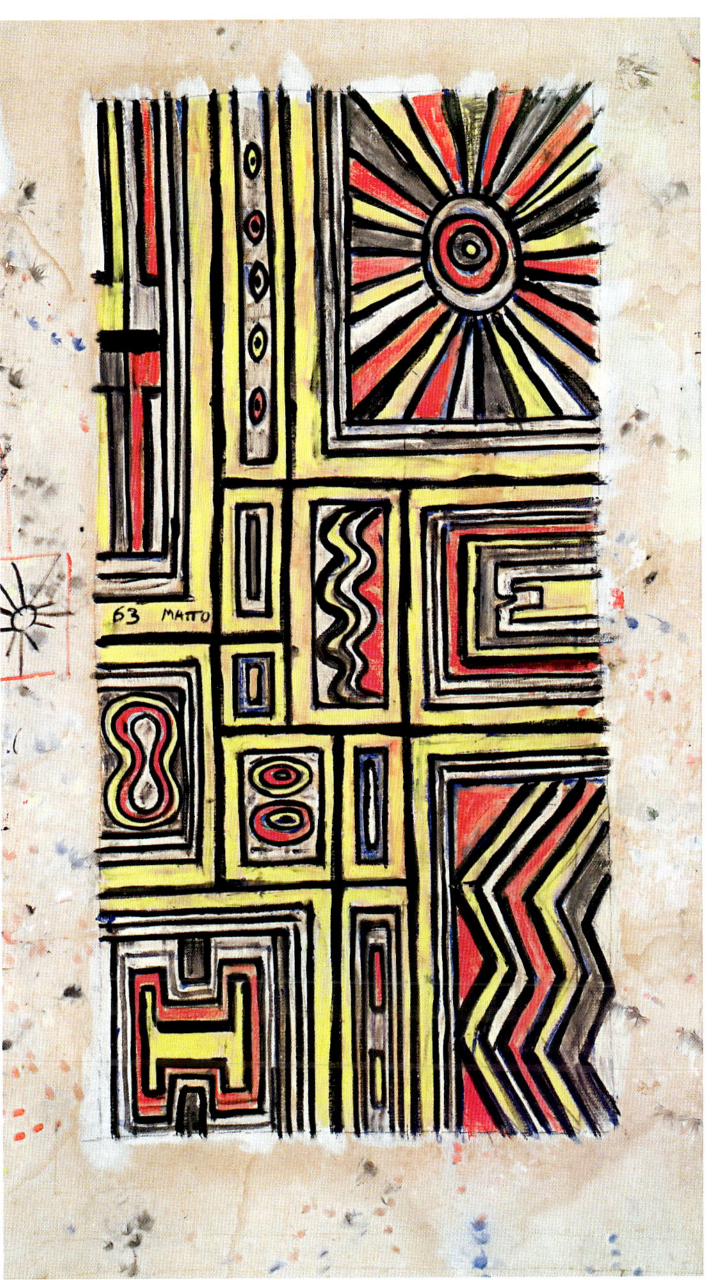
63 MATTO

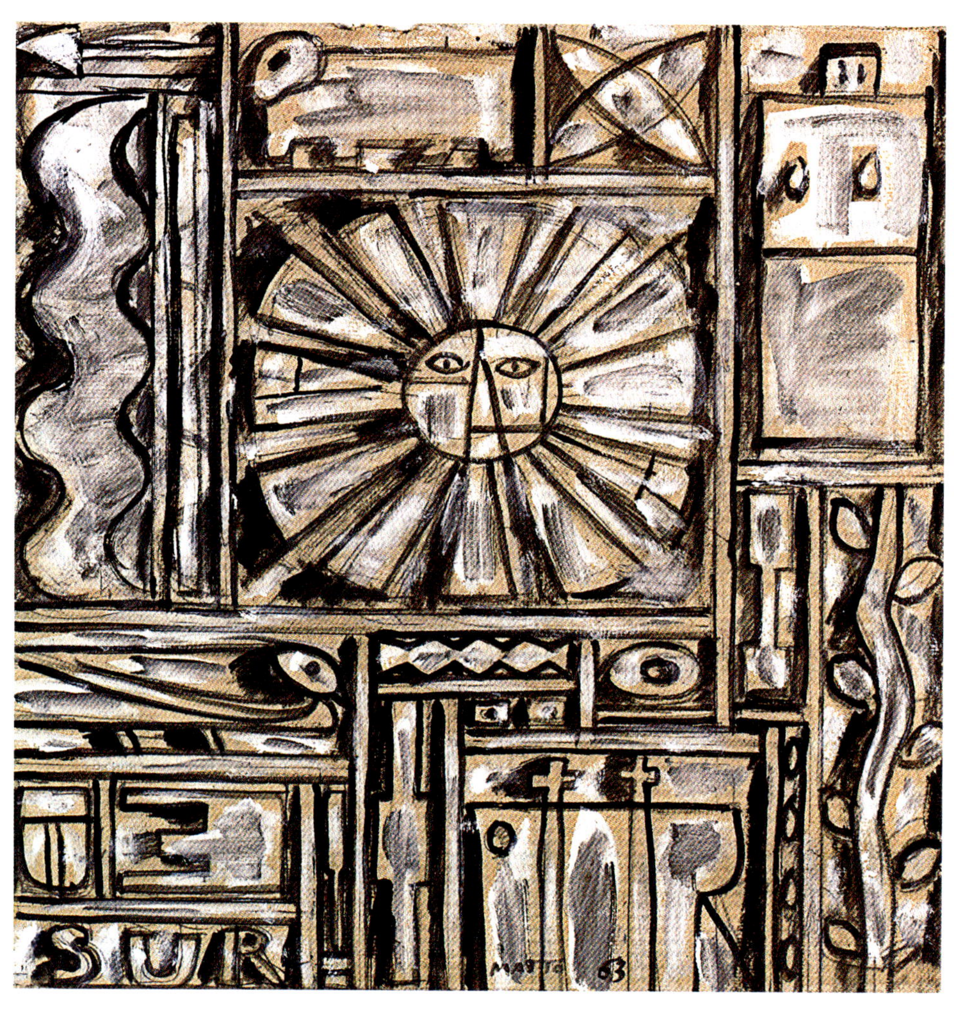

22   Sol [Sun] 1963; oil on wood; 23¾ × 23¾ inches. Private collection, Washington, D.C. Photo: Arturo Sánchez.

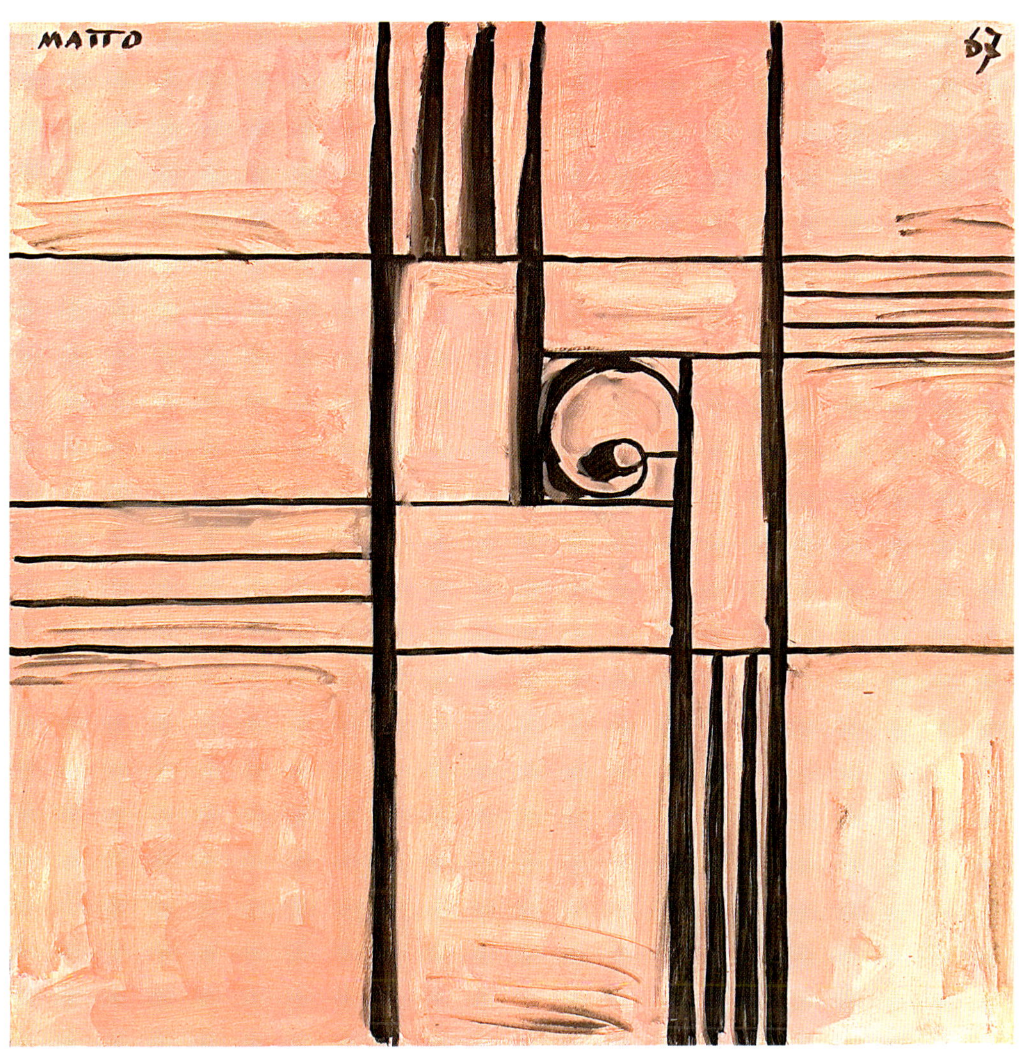

23 Constructivo rosa con caracol [Rose Constructive with Snail] 1967; oil on cardboard; 33⅛ × 33½ inches. Collection Estate of the Artist, Courtesy of Cecilia de Torres, Ltd. Photo: Arturo Sánchez.

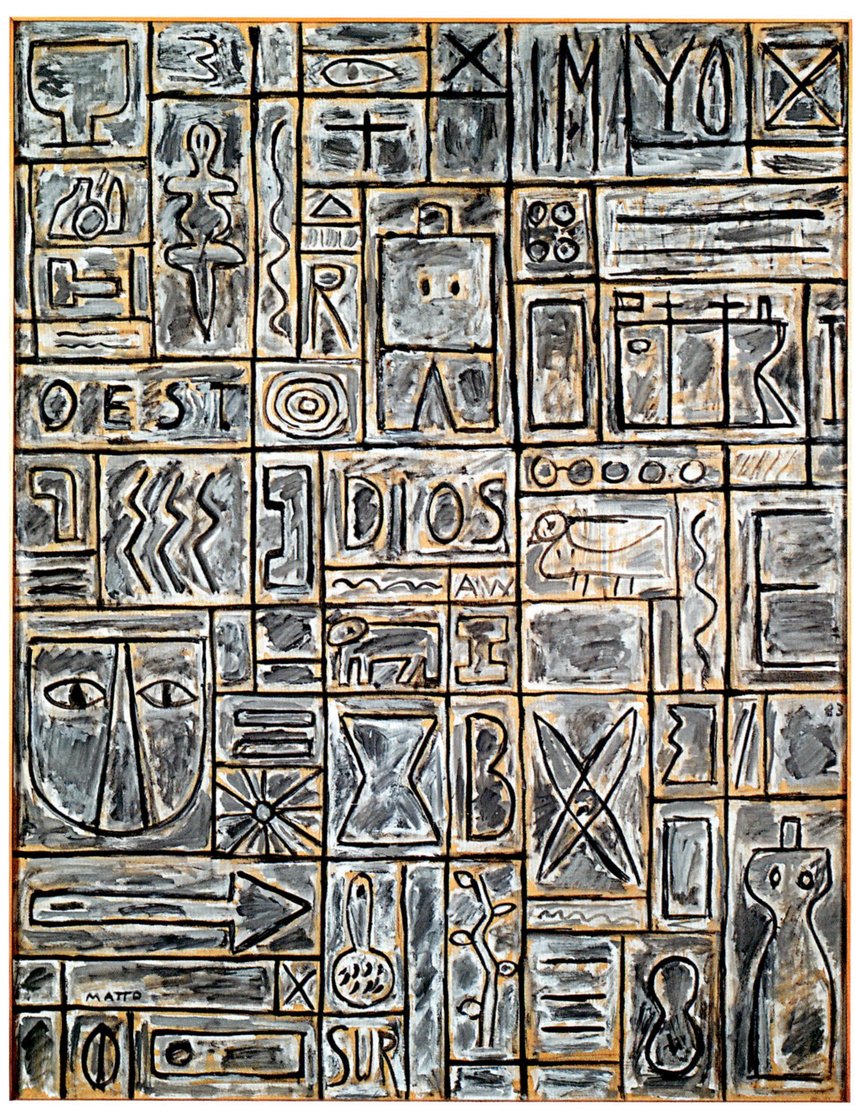

24 Constructivo [Constructive] 1983; oil on cardboard; 39 × 31⅛ inches. Private collection, Montevideo; Photo: Fábio Del Re – Vivafoto.

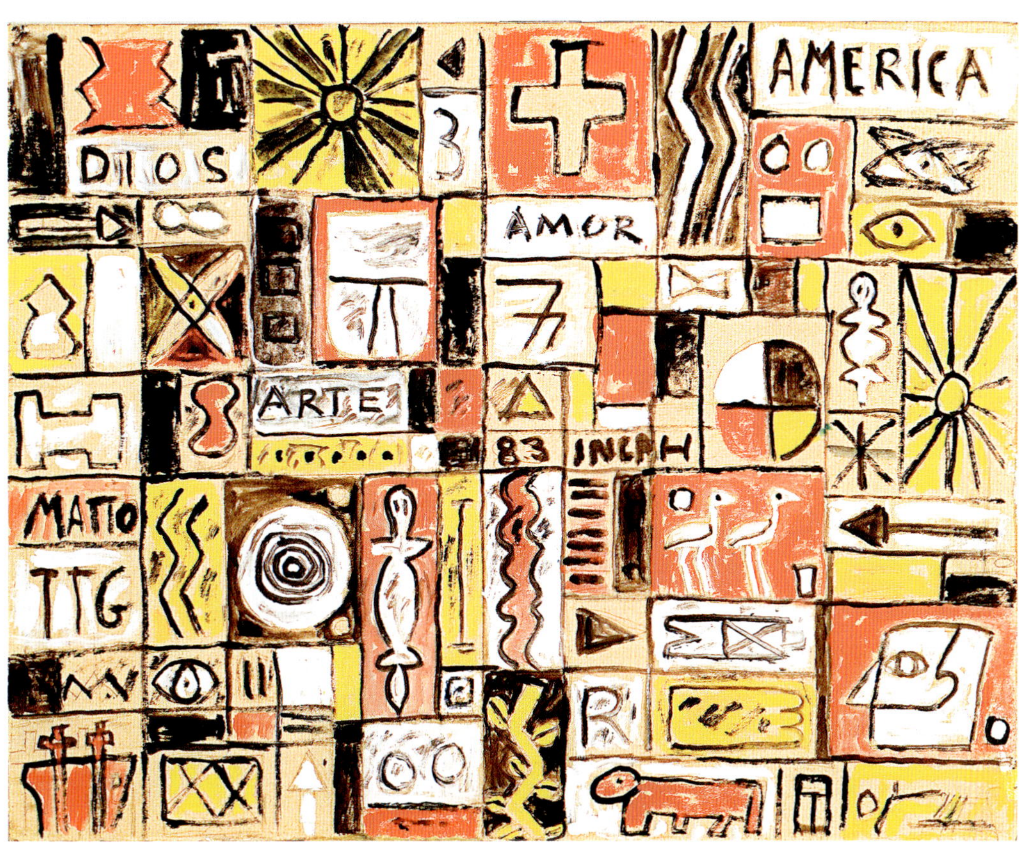

25 Constructivo América [America Constructive] 1983; oil on cardboard on canvas; 23 × 28⅛ inches. Collection Galería Oscar Prato, Montevideo. Photo: Fábio Del Re – Vivafoto.

Forms

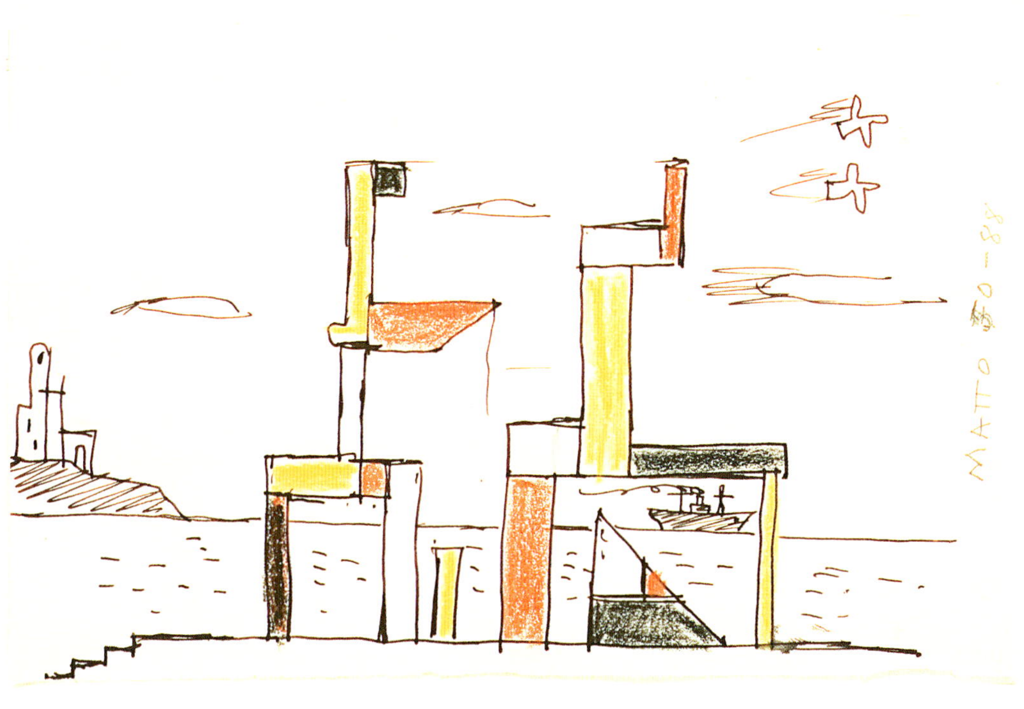

26   Dibujo para una escultura [Study for a Sculpture] 1950–1988; ink and crayon on paper; 6½ × 8 inches. Collection Estate of the Artist, Courtesy of Cecilia de Torres, Ltd. Photo: Arturo Sánchez.

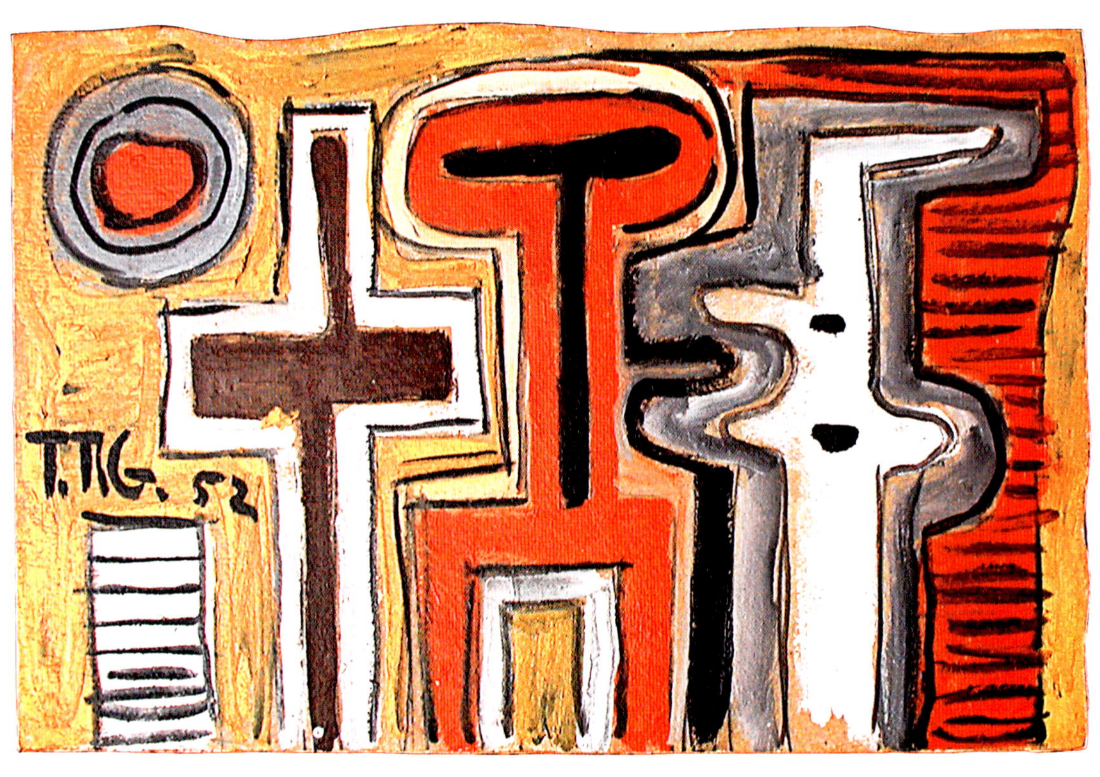

27   Sol y formas [Sun and Forms] 1952; oil on cardboard; 14 × 21 inches.
Private collection, Houston. Photo: Larry Lamay.

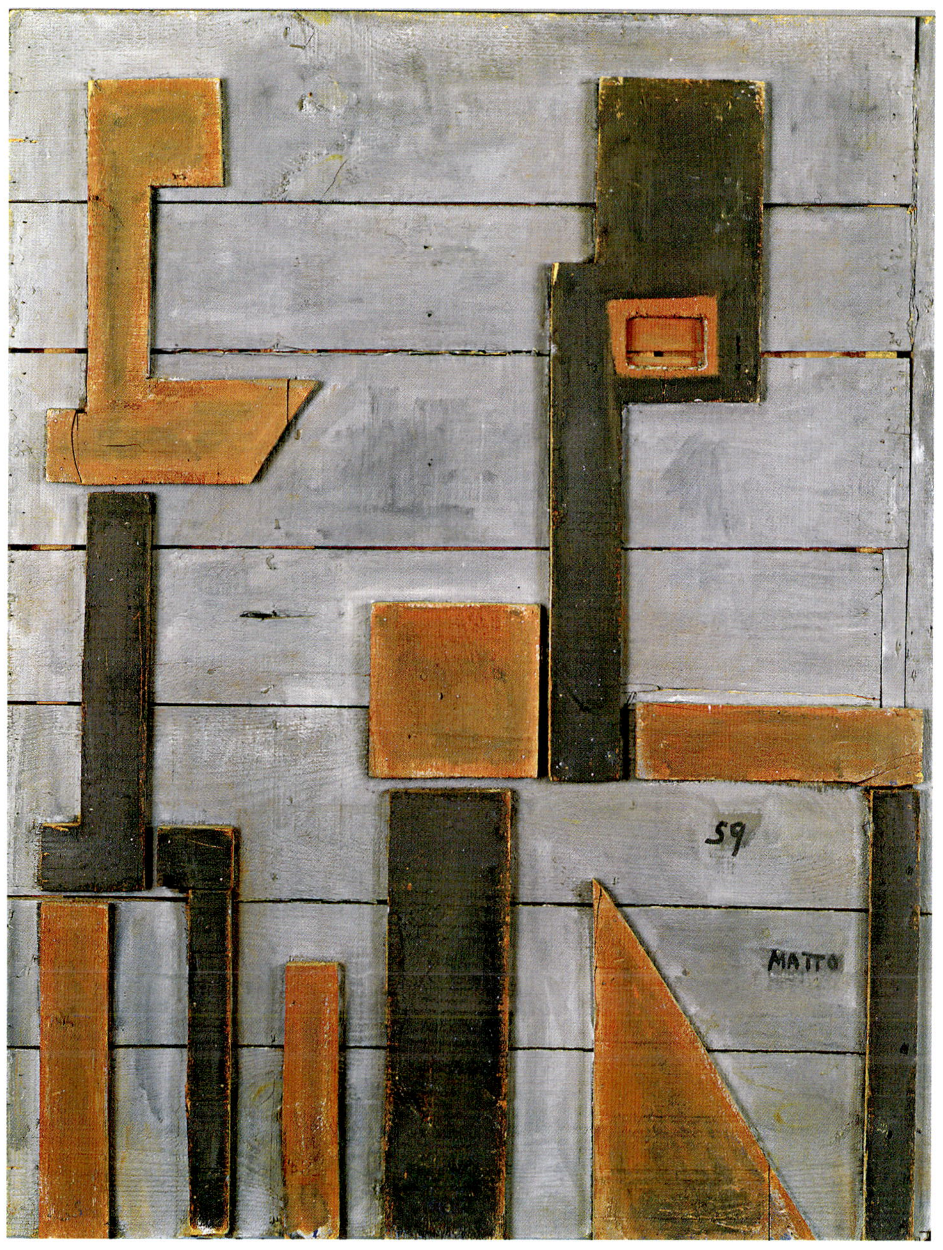

28 Dos formas [Two Forms] 1959; oil on wood; 41¼ × 31⅞ inches.
Collection Daniela Chappard Foundation. Photo: Arturo Sánchez.

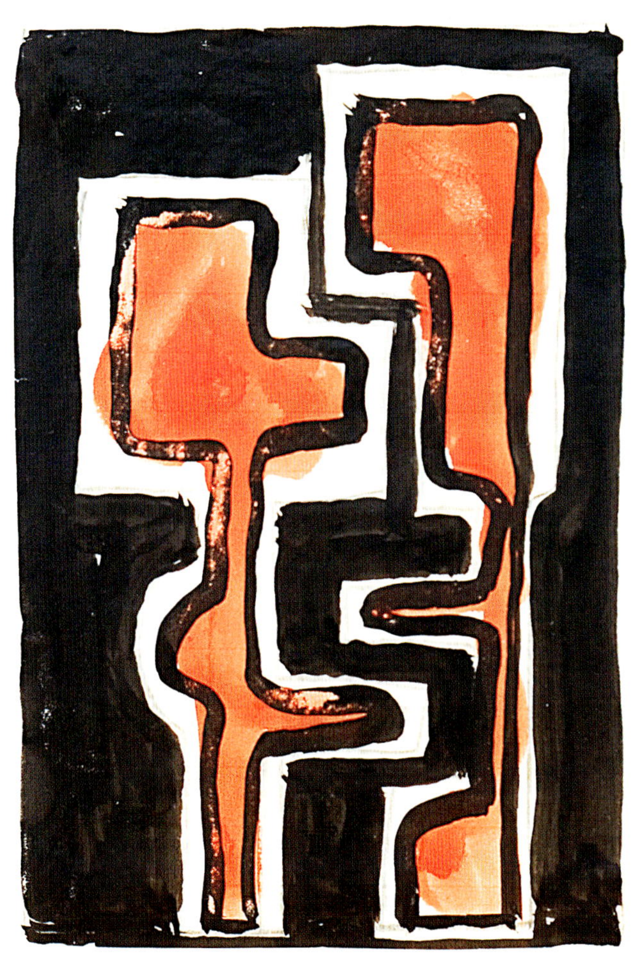

29 Dos formas en rojo [Two Forms in Red] 1960; pencil and watercolor on paper; 5¾ × 3¾ inches. Collection Estate of the Artist,
Courtesy of Cecilia de Torres, Ltd. Photo: Arturo Sánchez.

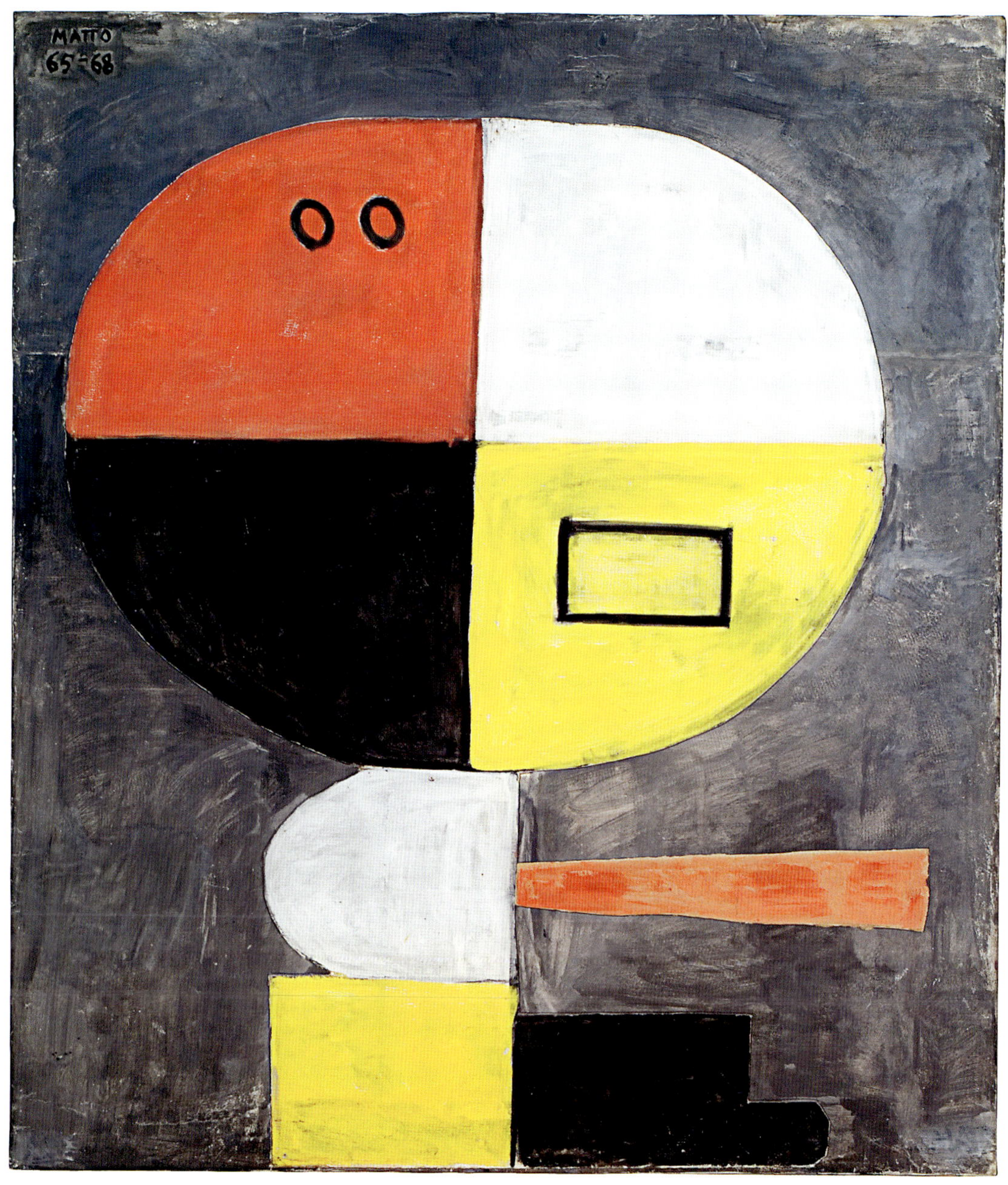

30   Veleta [Wind Vane] 1965–68; oil on cardboard on canvas;
46½ × 41 inches. Private collection, Montevideo. Photo:
Fábio Del Re – Vivafoto.

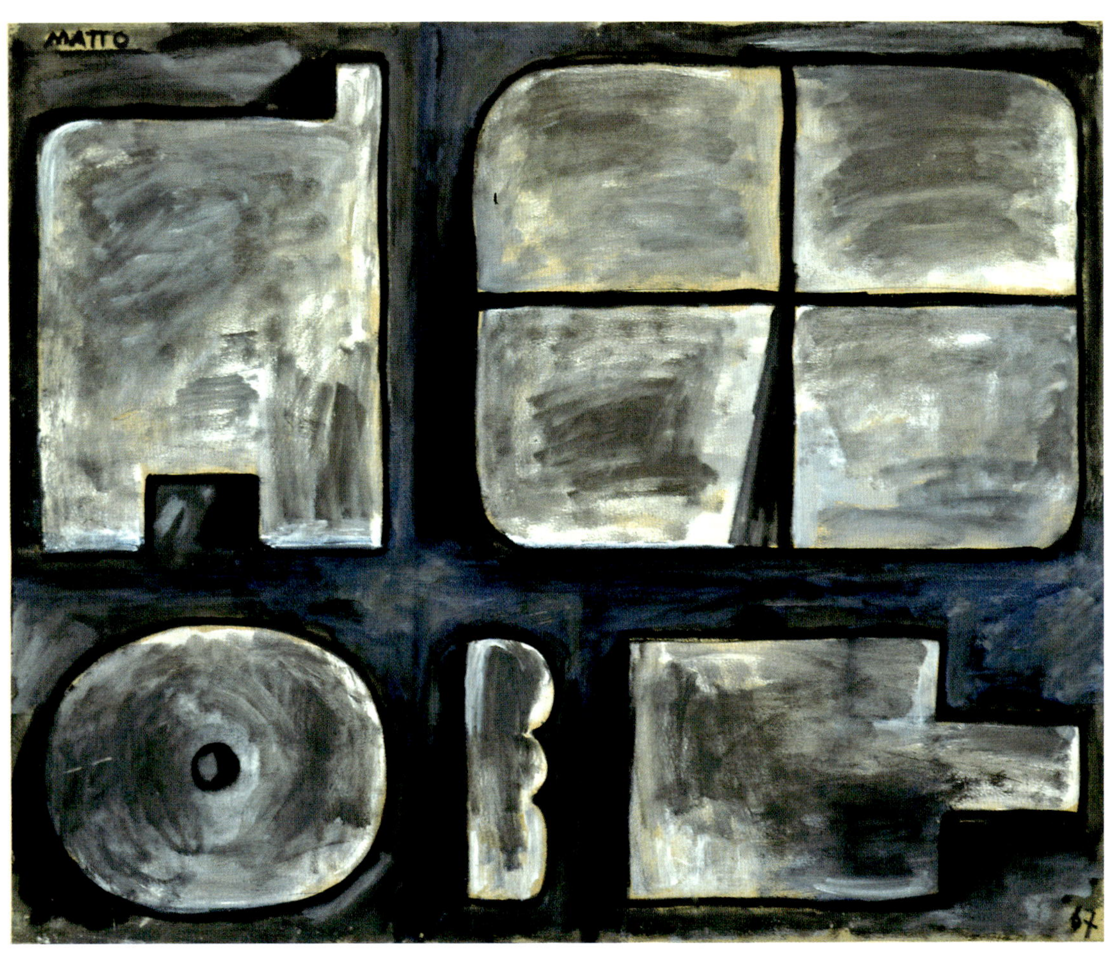

31   Cinco formas [Five Forms] 1967; oil on cardboard; 35⅝ × 44 inches.
Collection Lauren and Jeffrey Sugar.

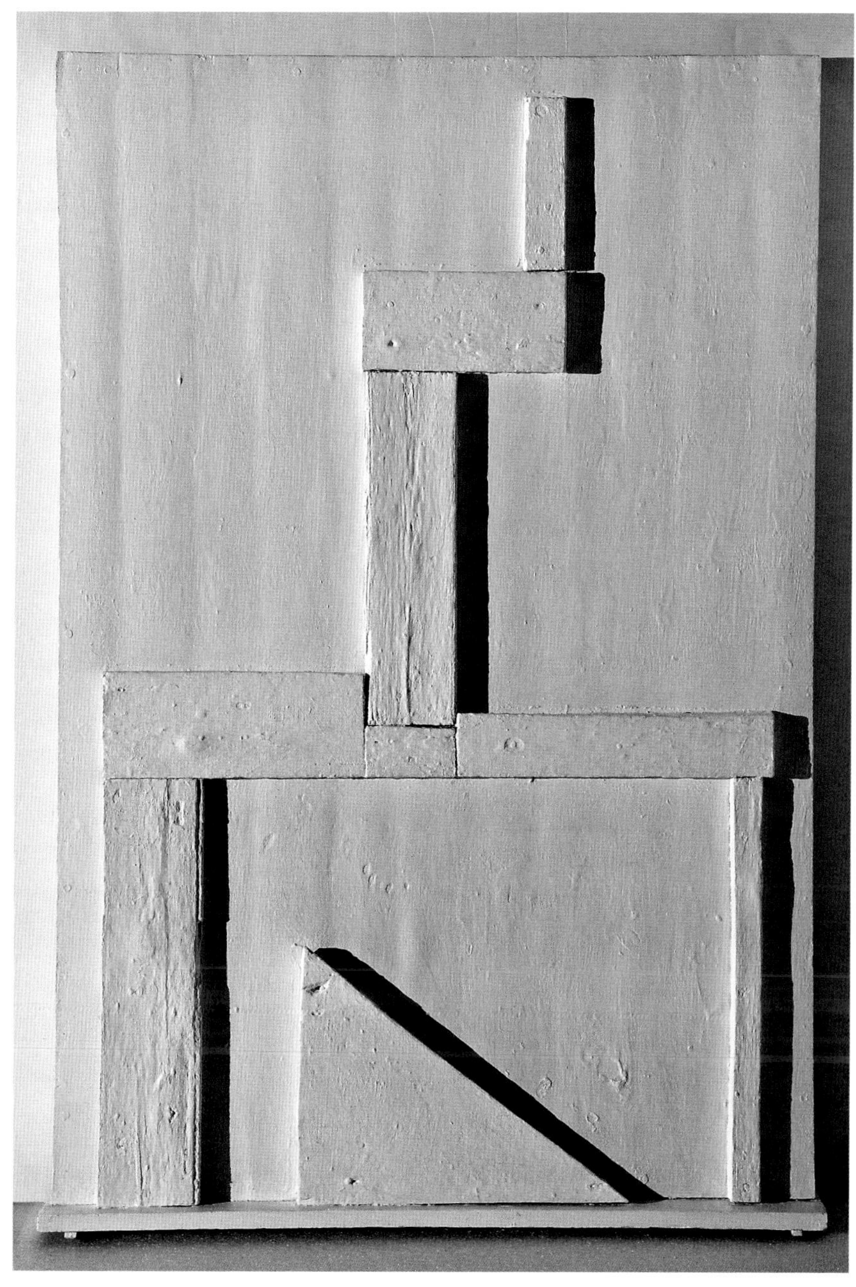

32 Forma blanca [White Form] c. 1970; oil on wood; 56¼ × 37½ inches.
Private collection, New York, Courtesy of Cecilia de Torres, Ltd.
Photo: Arturo Sánchez.

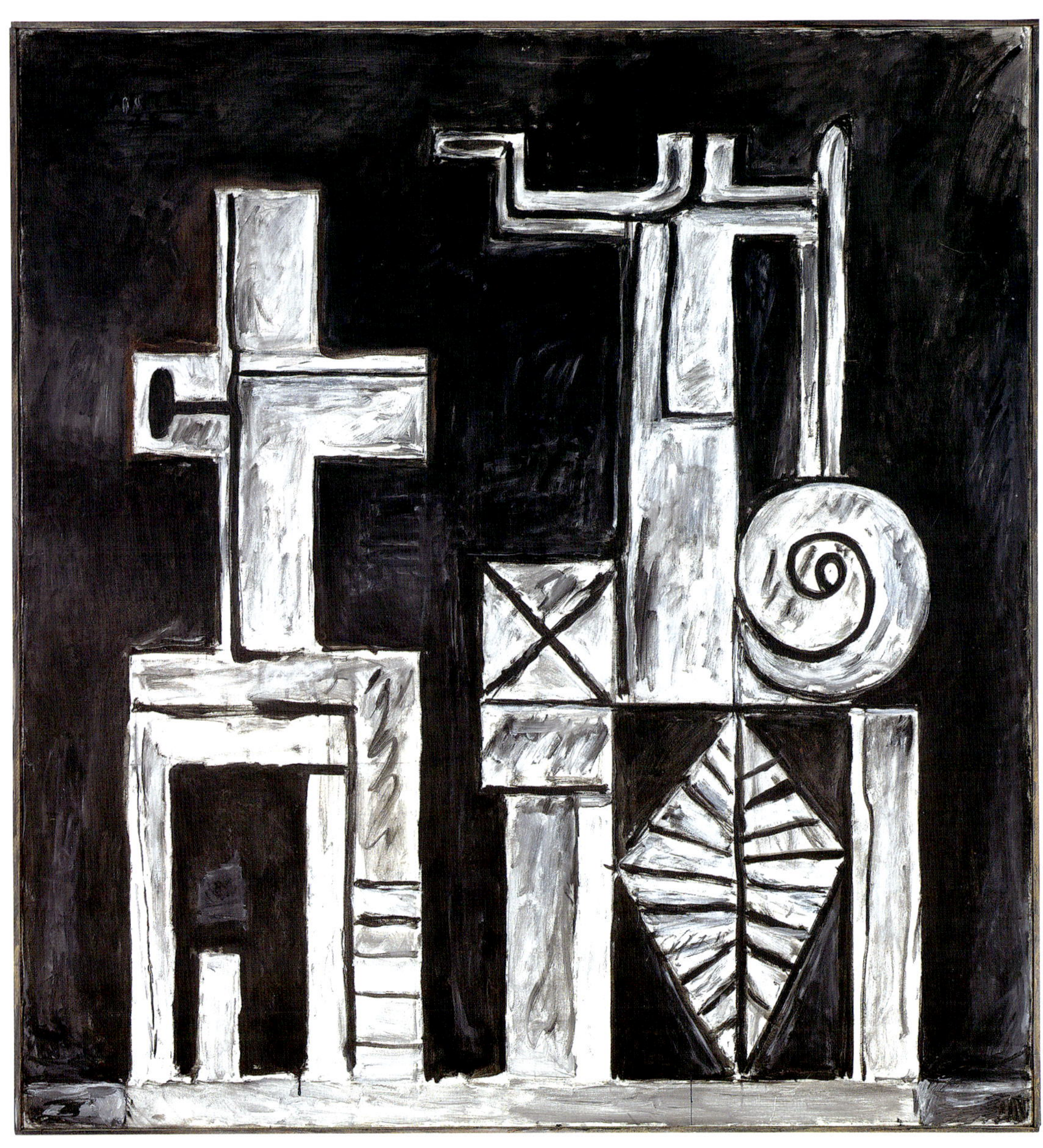

33 Formas [Forms] 1974; oil on canvas; 61 × 57 7/8 inches.
Private collection. Photo: Hugo Maertens.

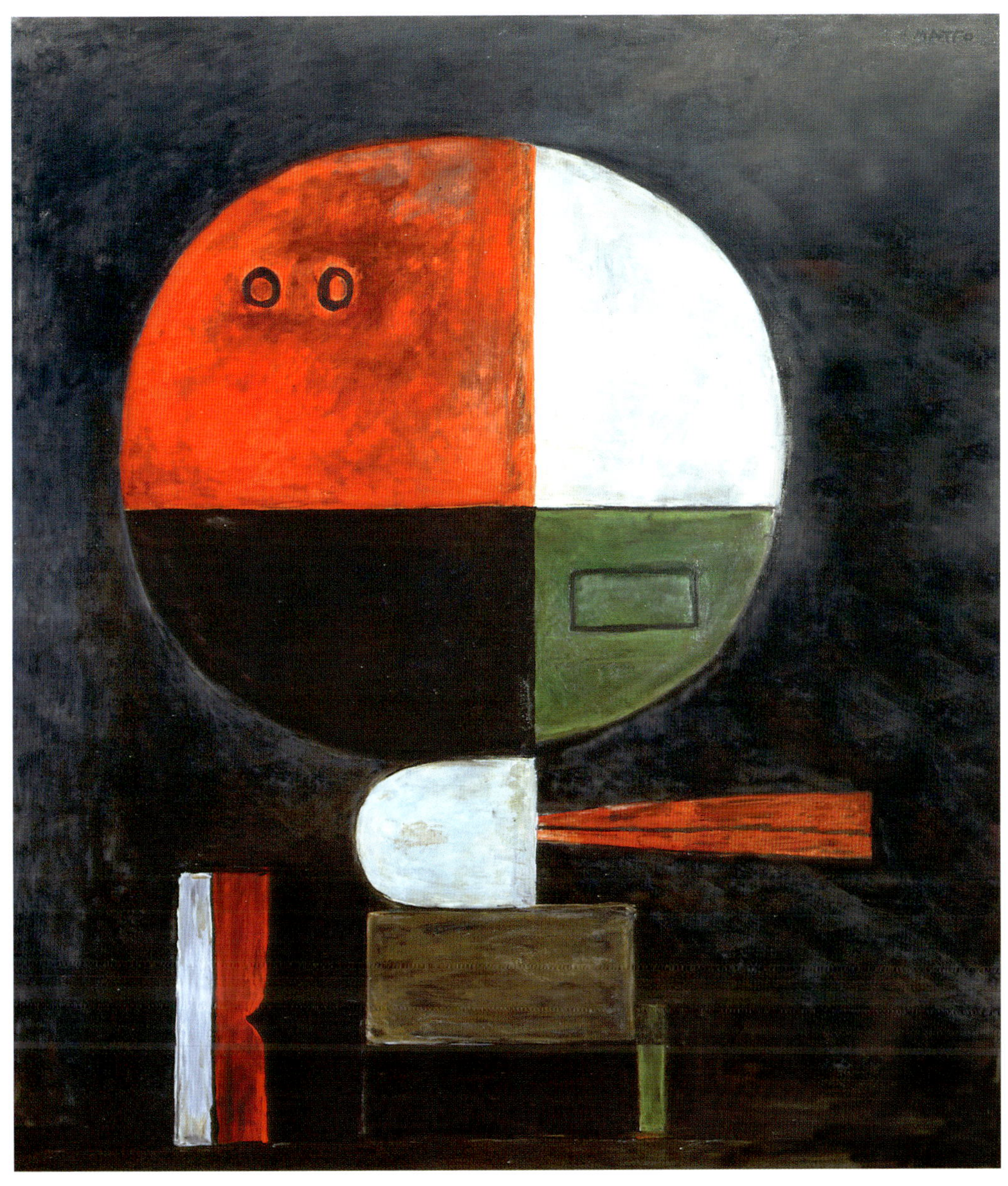

34   Veleta [Wind Vane] 1974; oil on canvas; $21\frac{3}{8} \times 17\frac{5}{8}$ inches.
Collection Estate of the Artist, Courtesy of Cecilia de Torres, Ltd.
Photo: Arturo Sánchez.

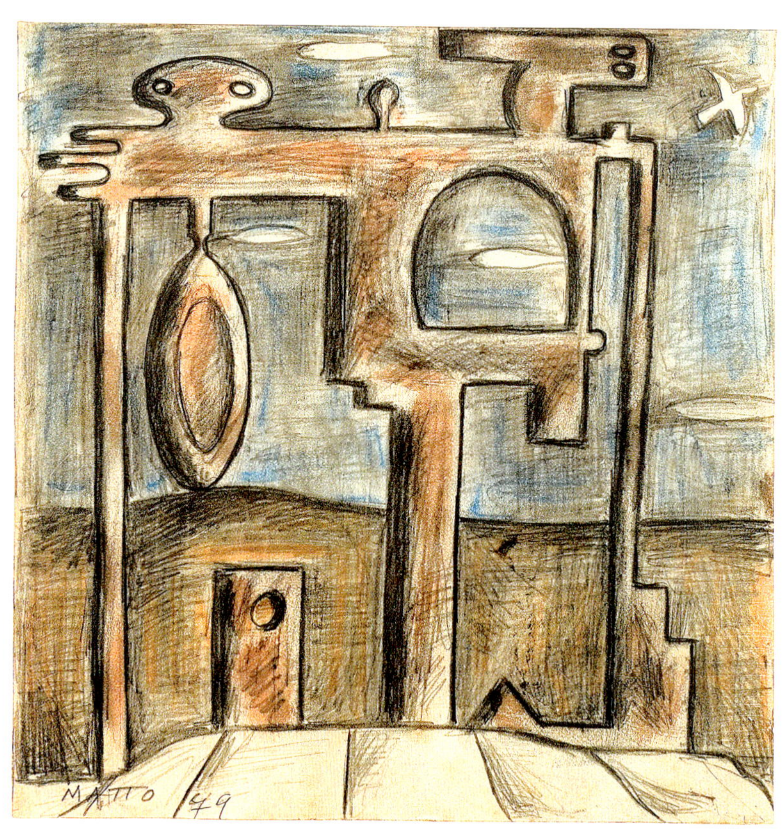

35 Formas proyecto de monumento [Project for Monument Forms] 1979; crayon and watercolor on paper; 8½ × 8½ inches. Collection Estate of the Artist, Courtesy of Cecilia de Torres, Ltd. Photo: Arturo Sánchez.

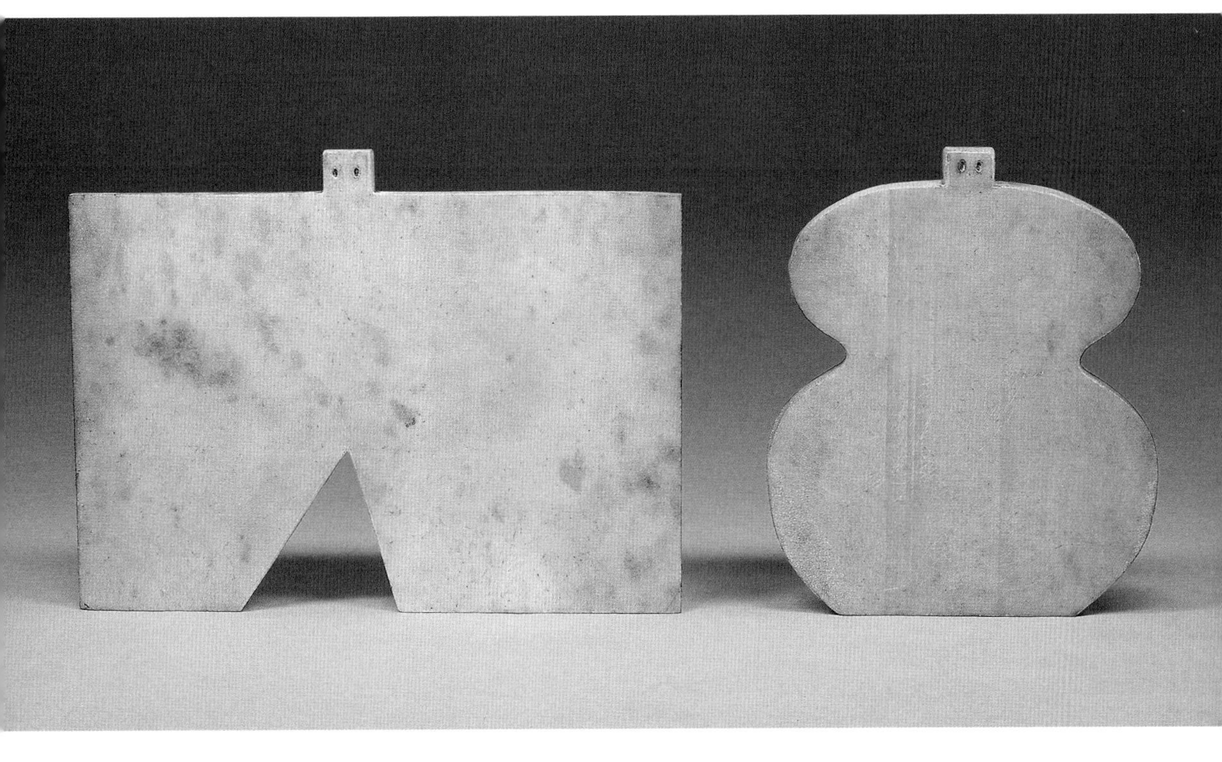

36   Pareja [Couple] c. 1982; marble; 19⁵/₁₆ × 25⁹/₁₆ inches.
Colección Patricia Phelps de Cisneros. Photo: Mark Morosse.

Woods

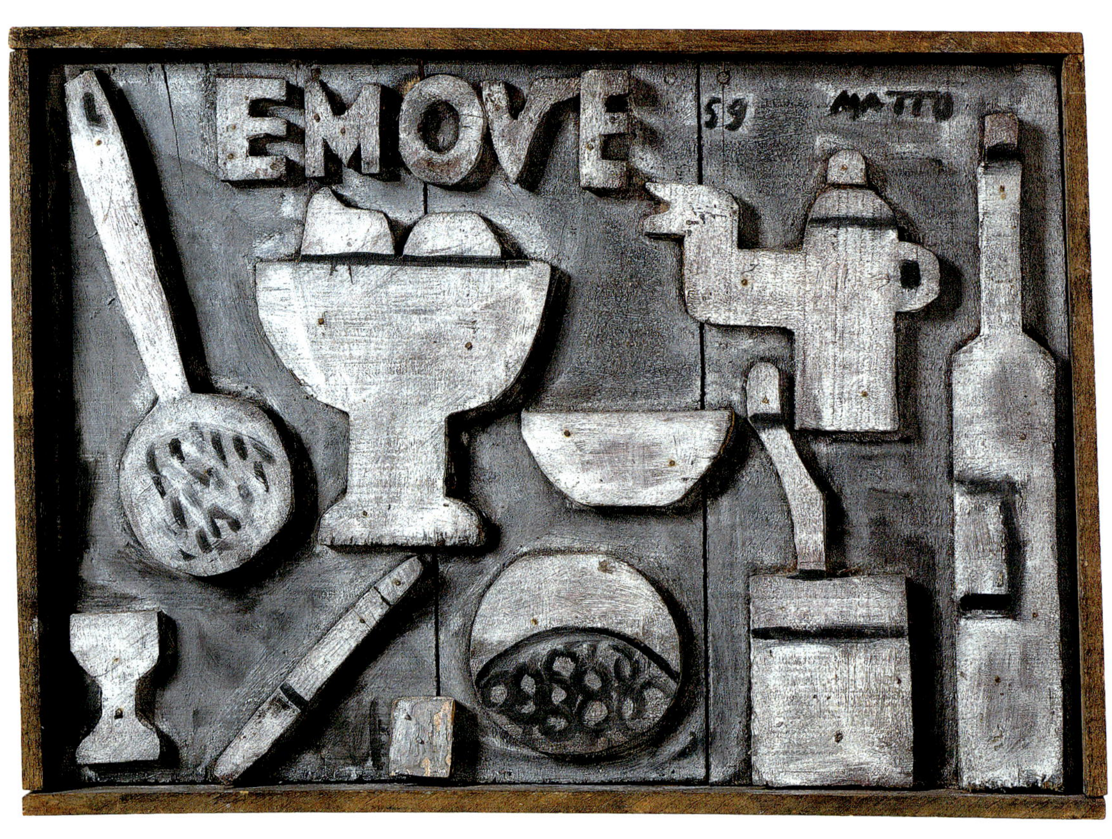

37 Removedor—Relieve [Removedor—Relief] 1959; oil on wood; 15 × 20⅞ inches. Collection Estate of the Artist, Courtesy of Cecilia de Torres, Ltd. Photo: Larry Lamay.

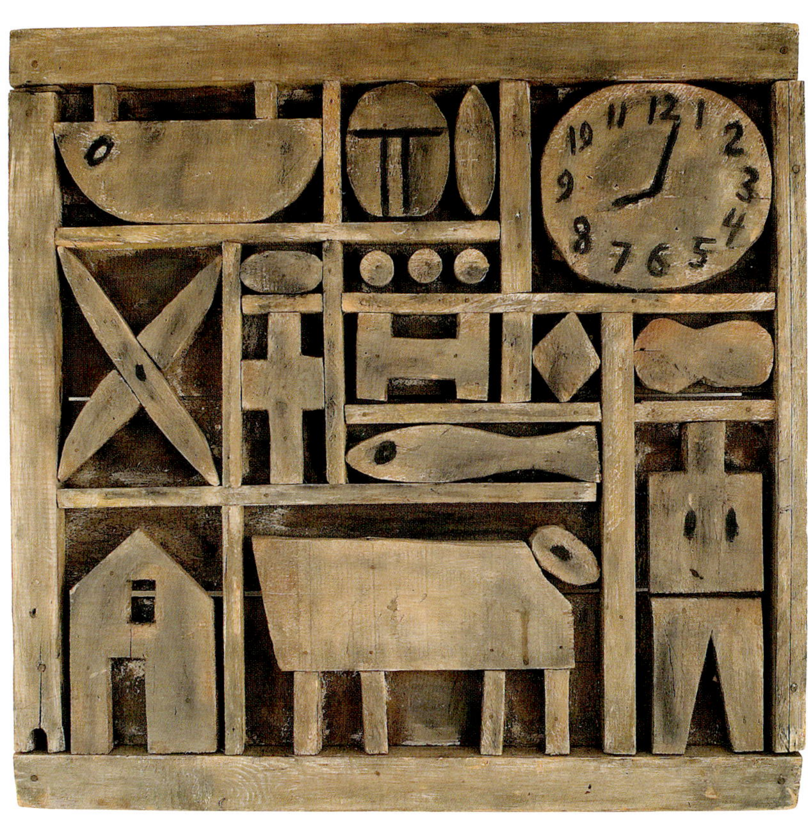

38 Construcción en madera [Construction in Wood] c. 1960; oil on wood; 23¼ × 24¼ inches. Private collection, Miami. Photo: Arturo Sánchez.

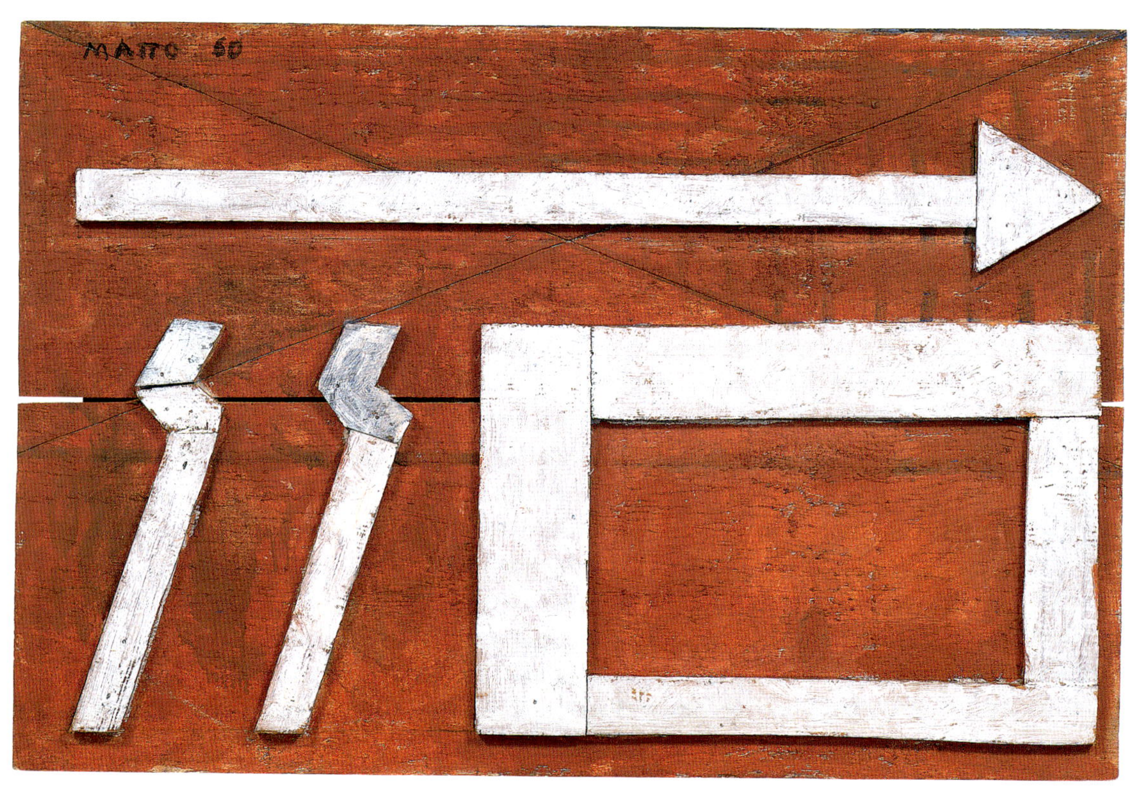

39   Flecha blanca [White Arrow] 1960; oil on wood; 23¹⁄₄ × 35³⁄₈ inches.
Collection Estate of the Artist, Courtesy of Cecilia de Torres, Ltd.
Photo: Larry Lamay.

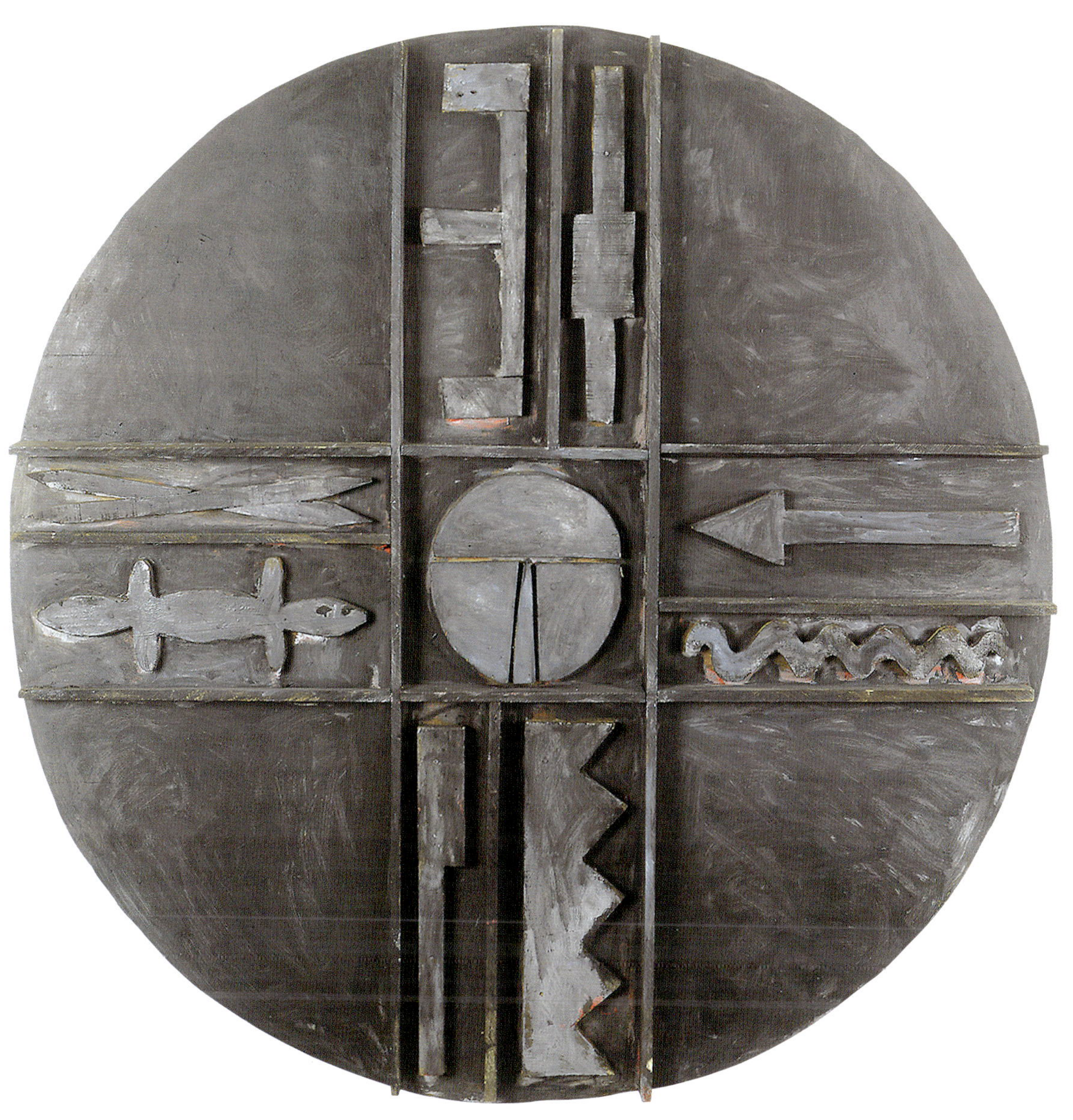

40 Construcción redonda [Round Construction] 1965–1980; oil on wood; $52^{3}/_{8} \times 52^{3}/_{8} \times 3^{1}/_{2}$ inches. Collection Daniela Chappard Foundation. Photo: Courtesy of Cecilia de Torres.

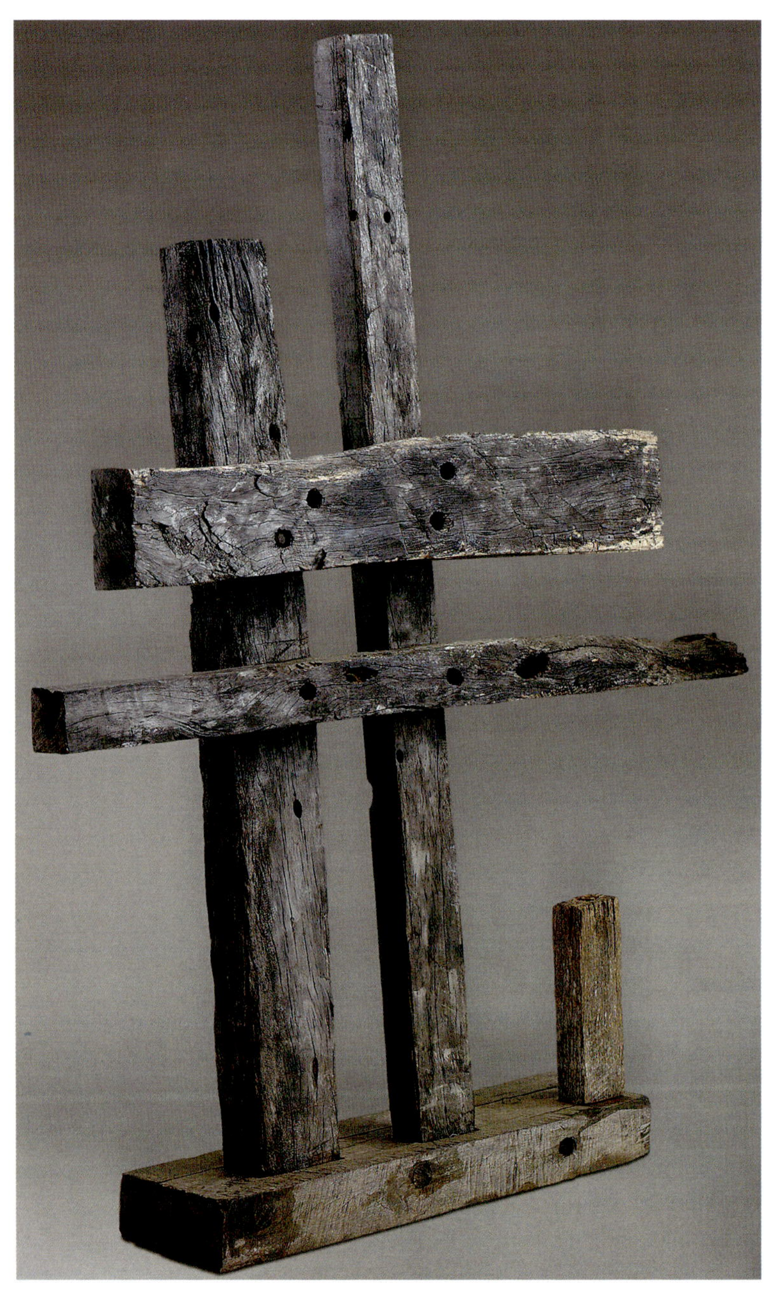

41   Monumento en quebracho [Monument in Quebracho Wood]
c. 1965; wood; 55⅞ × 44⅞ × 7½ inches. Private collection.
Photo: Hugo Maertens.

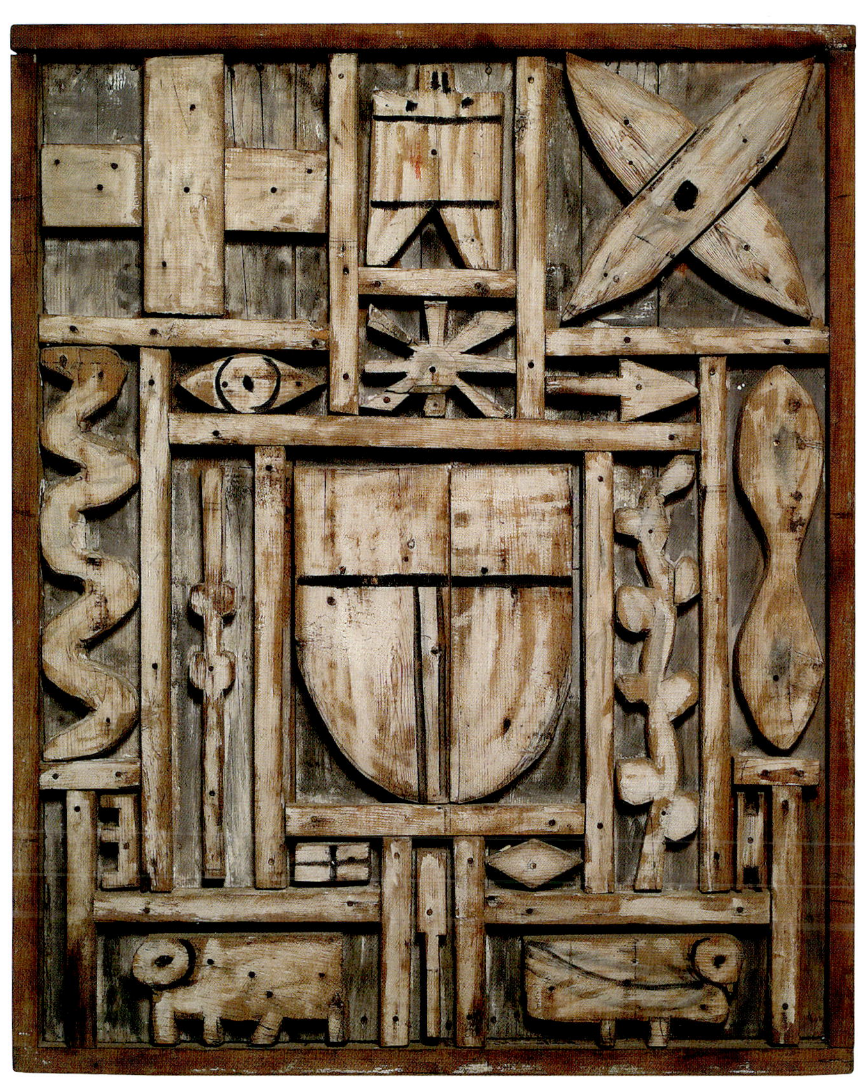

42 Constructivo con máscara [Constructive with Mask] c. 1968;
oil on wood; 36⅜ × 29¾ inches. Private collection, Montevideo.
Photo: Fábio Del Re – Vivafoto.

43   Venus rosa [Rose Venus] 1979; oil on wood; 81⅞ inches (height). Collection Susan and Mac Dunwoody, Houston.

U 1970; oil on wood; 84 inches (height). Collection Susan and Mac Dunwoody, Houston.

Azul y blanco [Blue and White] n.d.; oil on wood; 91¼ inches (height). Collection Susan and Mac Dunwoody, Houston.

Photo: Arturo Sánchez.

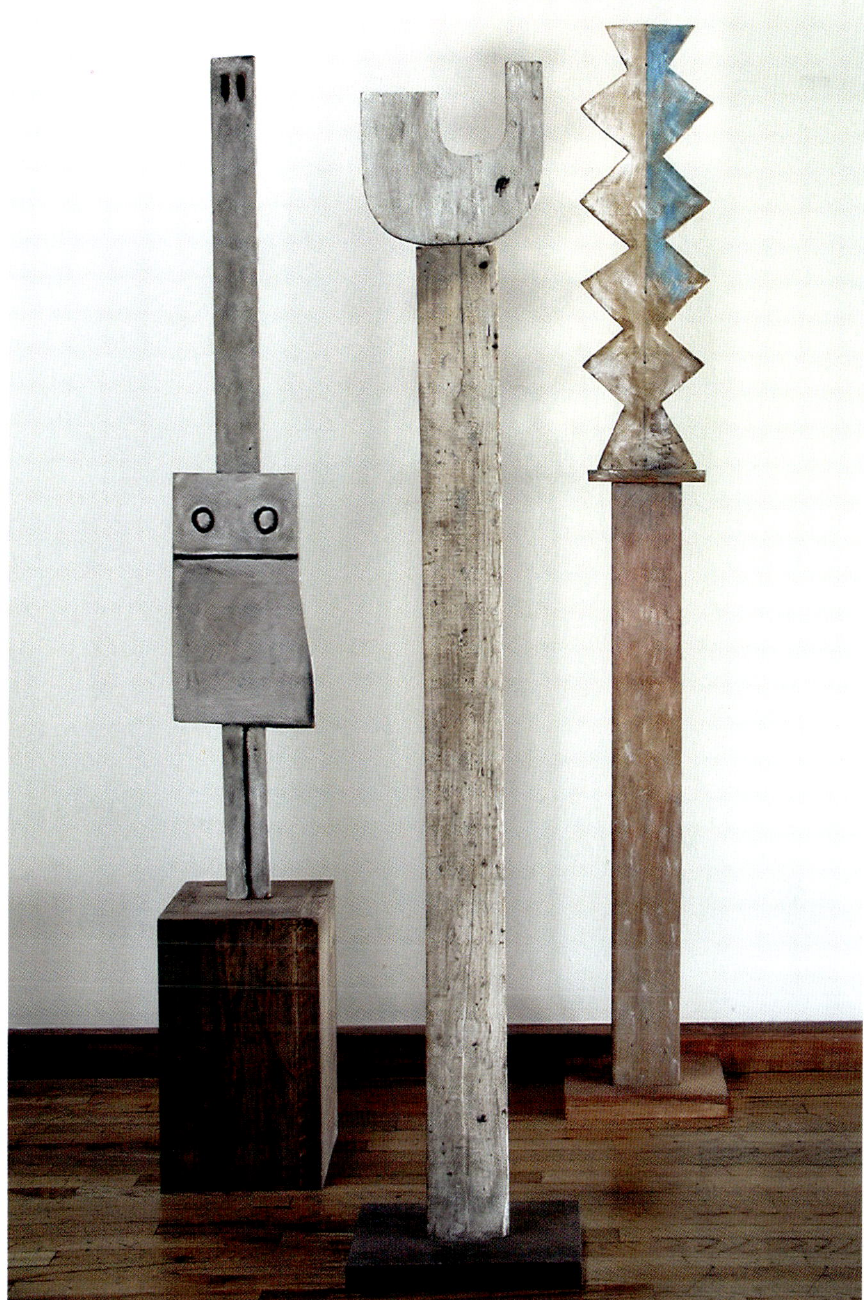

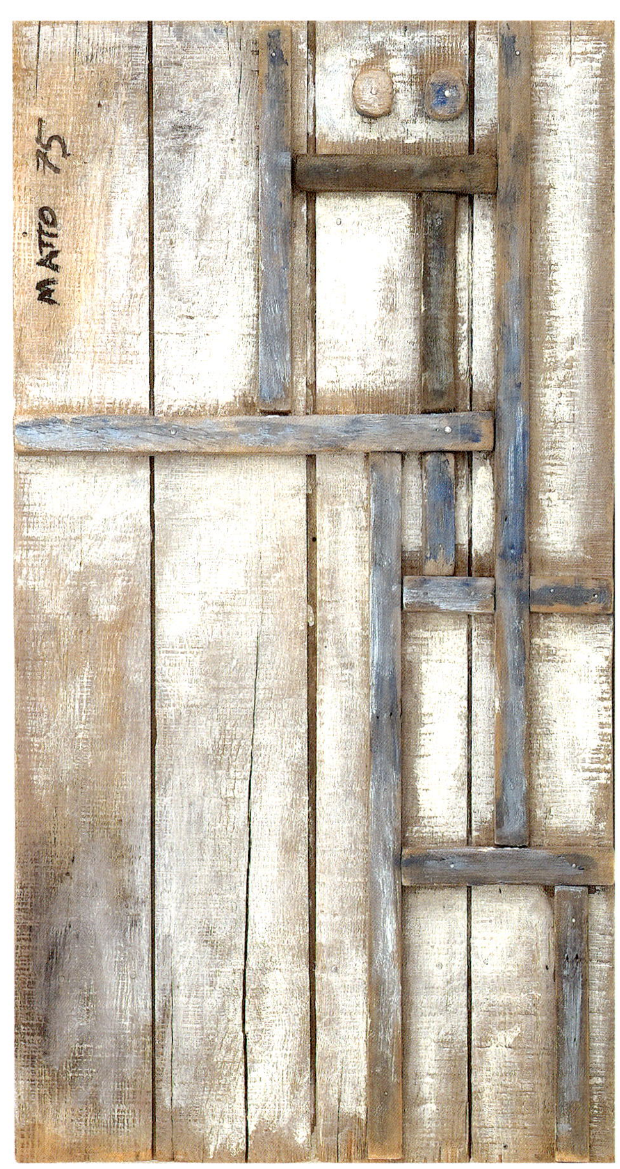

44   Construcción en blanco y celeste—Relieve [Construction in
       White and Sky Blue—Relief] 1975; oil on wood; 23¼ × 13⅜ inches.
       Collection Estate of the Artist, Courtesy of Cecilia de Torres, Ltd.
       Photo: Arturo Sánchez.

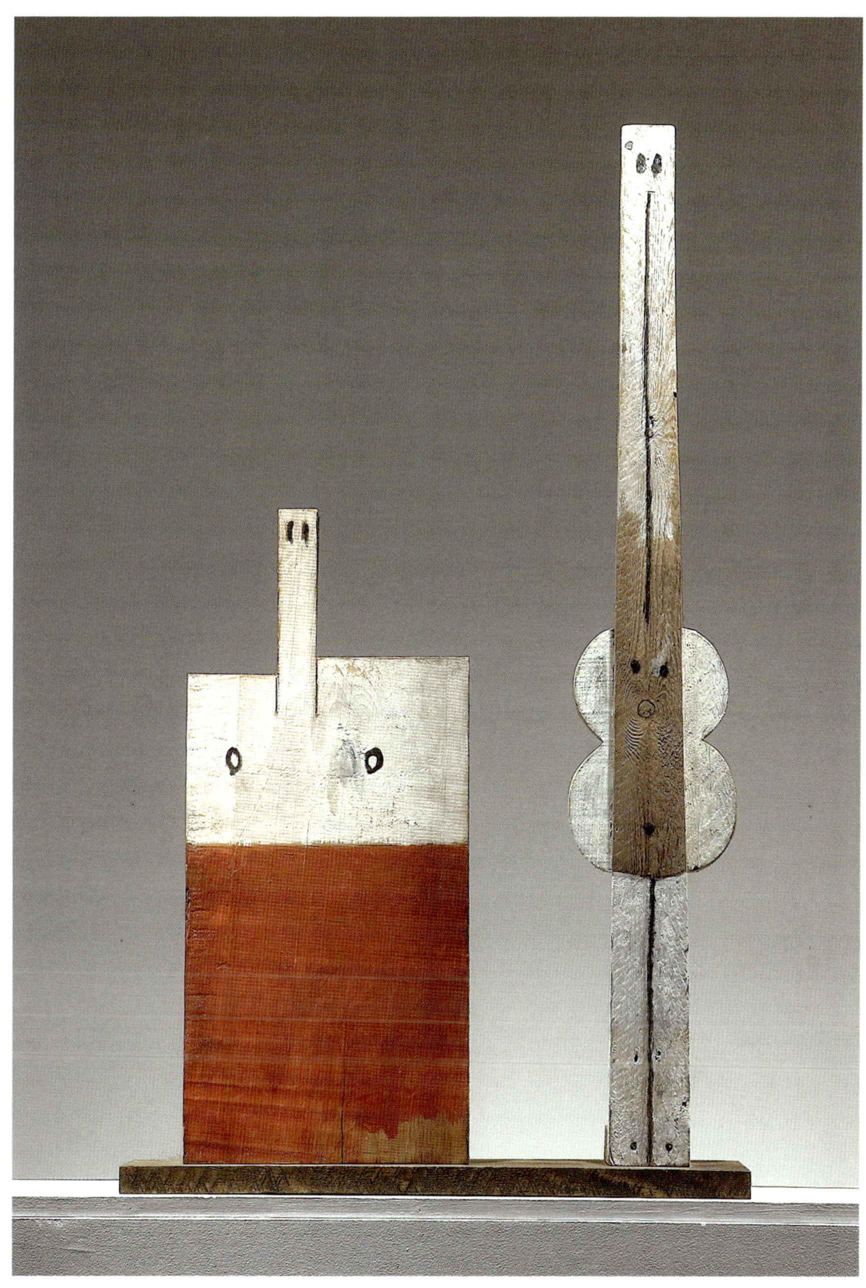

45   Dos Venus [Two Venuses] 1976; oil on wood; 44⅞ × 26⅜ × 6¾ inches. Collection Estate of the Artist, Courtesy of Cecilia de Torres, Ltd. Photo: Arturo Sánchez.

46   Monumento [Monument] 1979; oil on wood; 89³/₈ × 83¹/₂ × 13³/₄ inches.
Private collection. Photo: Hugo Maertens.

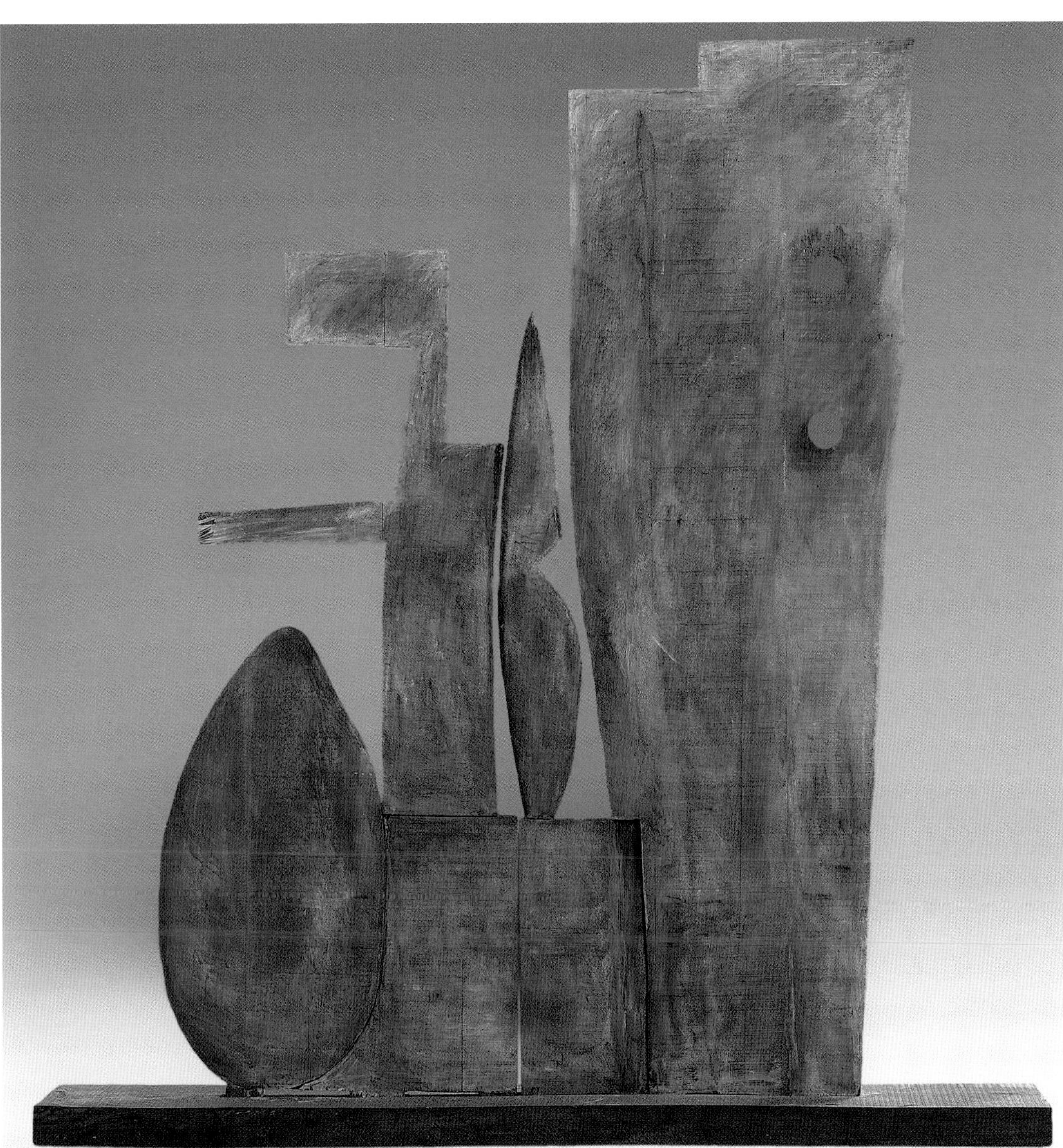

47 Venus 1979; oil on wood; 81⅞ × 10¾ inches. The Museum of Fine Arts, Houston, Gift of Alfred C. Glassell III and Marli Andrade, Mary and Roy Cullen, Marjorie H. Wortham, Joanna and Richard W. Wortham III, and the Caroline Wiess Law Foundation.

Caracol grande [Large Snail] 1985; oil on wood; 64 × 12 × 11 inches. The Museum of Fine Arts, Houston, Gift of Alfred C. Glassell III and Marli Andrade, Mary and Roy Cullen, Marjorie H. Wortham, Joanna and Richard W. Wortham III, and the Caroline Wiess Law Foundation.

Venus blanquiazul [White and Blue Venus] 1980; oil on wood; 96 × 13¾ × 12 inches. The Museum of Fine Arts, Houston, Gift of Alfred C. Glassell III and Marli Andrade, Mary and Roy Cullen, Marjorie H. Wortham, Joanna and Richard W. Wortham III, and the Caroline Wiess Law Foundation.

Cordero [Lamb] c. 1979; oil on wood; 70¼ × 15½ × 4¾ inches. The Museum of Fine Arts, Houston, Gift of Ada Antuña de Matto.

Máscara [Mask] 1979; oil on wood; 82½ × 9¼ × 5¾ inches. The Museum of Fine Arts, Houston, Gift of Alfred C. Glassell III and Marli Andrade, Mary and Roy Cullen, Marjorie H. Wortham, Joanna and Richard W. Wortham III, and the Caroline Wiess Law Foundation.

© The Museum of Fine Arts, Houston. Photo: Thomas R. DuBrock.

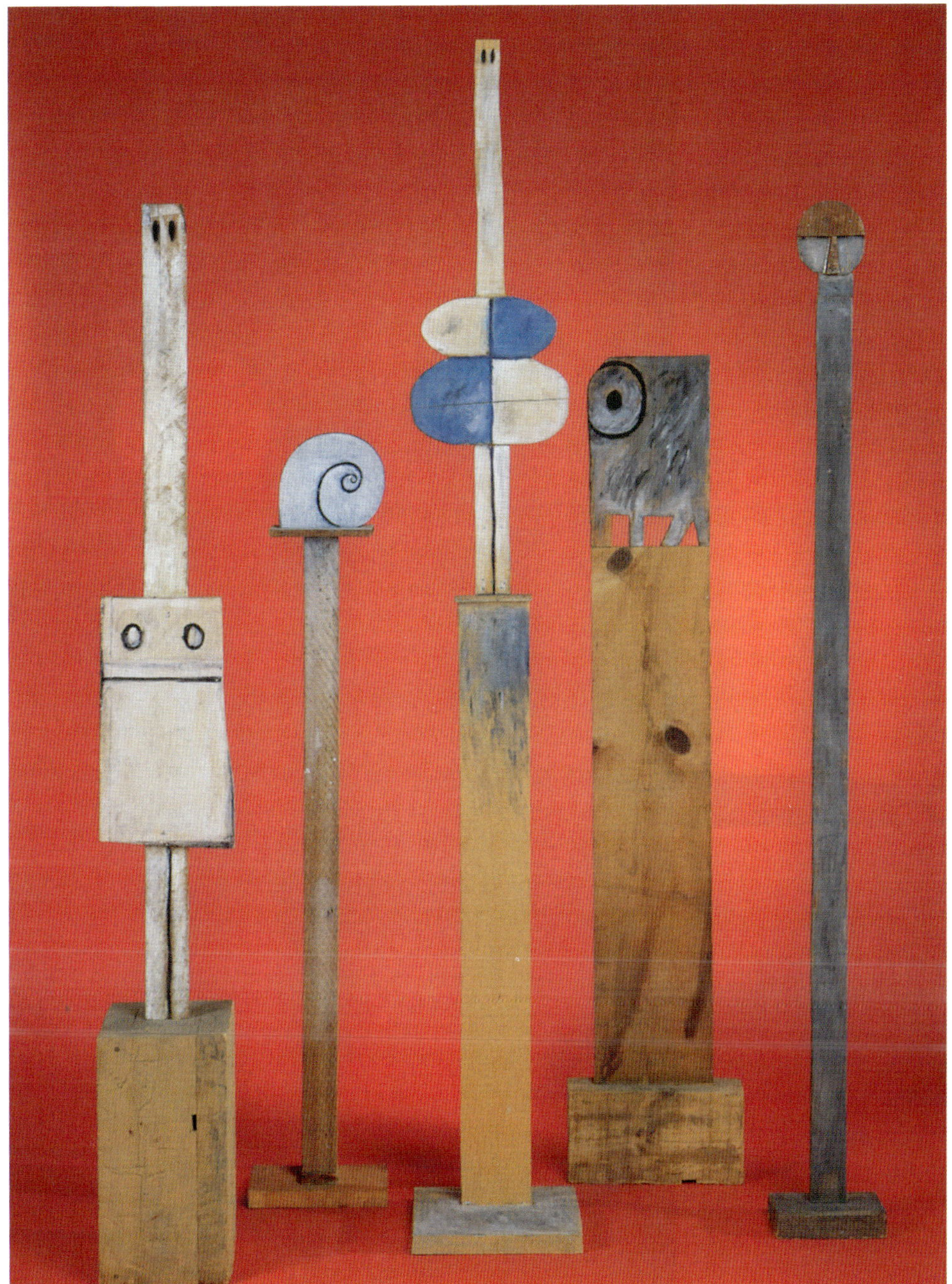

  1980; oil on wood; 77½ × 29½ × 2 inches. Private collection. Photo: Hugo Maertens.

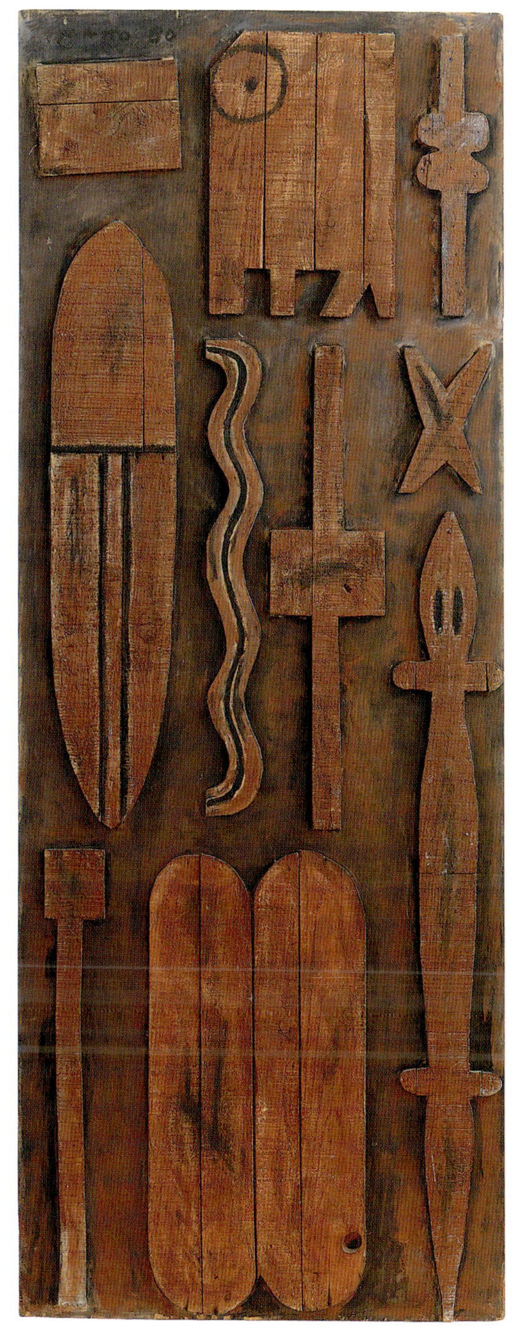

49 Hombre universal [Universal Man] 1988; oil on wood; 83 inches (height). Collection Estate of the Artist, Courtesy of Cecilia de Torres, Ltd. Photo: Arturo Sánchez.

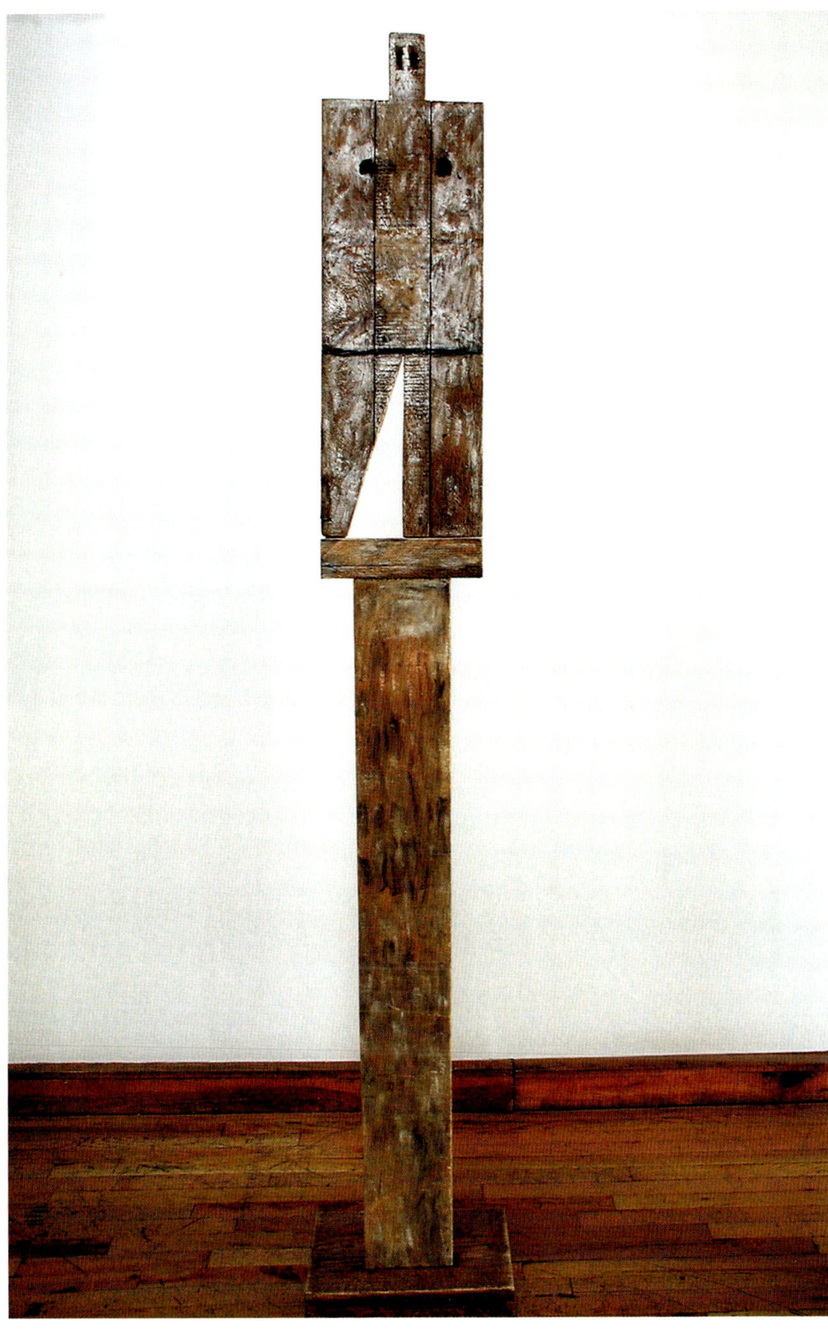

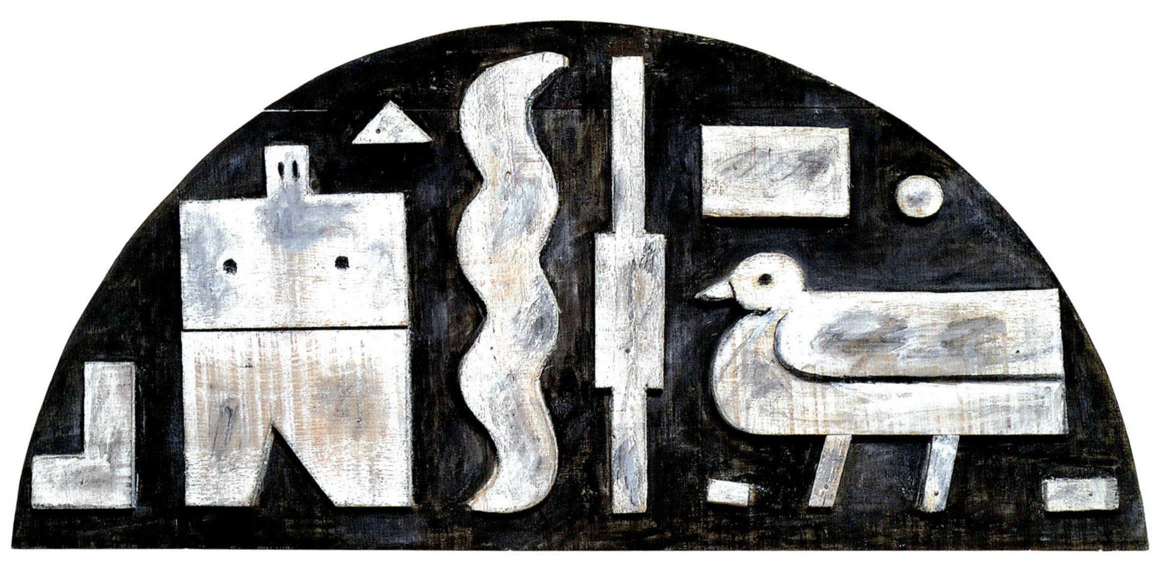

 Dintel [Lintel] 1988; oil on wood; 24 × 3¾ × 3¾ inches. Collection Judy and Charles Tate, Houston. Photo: Fábio Del Re – Vivafoto.

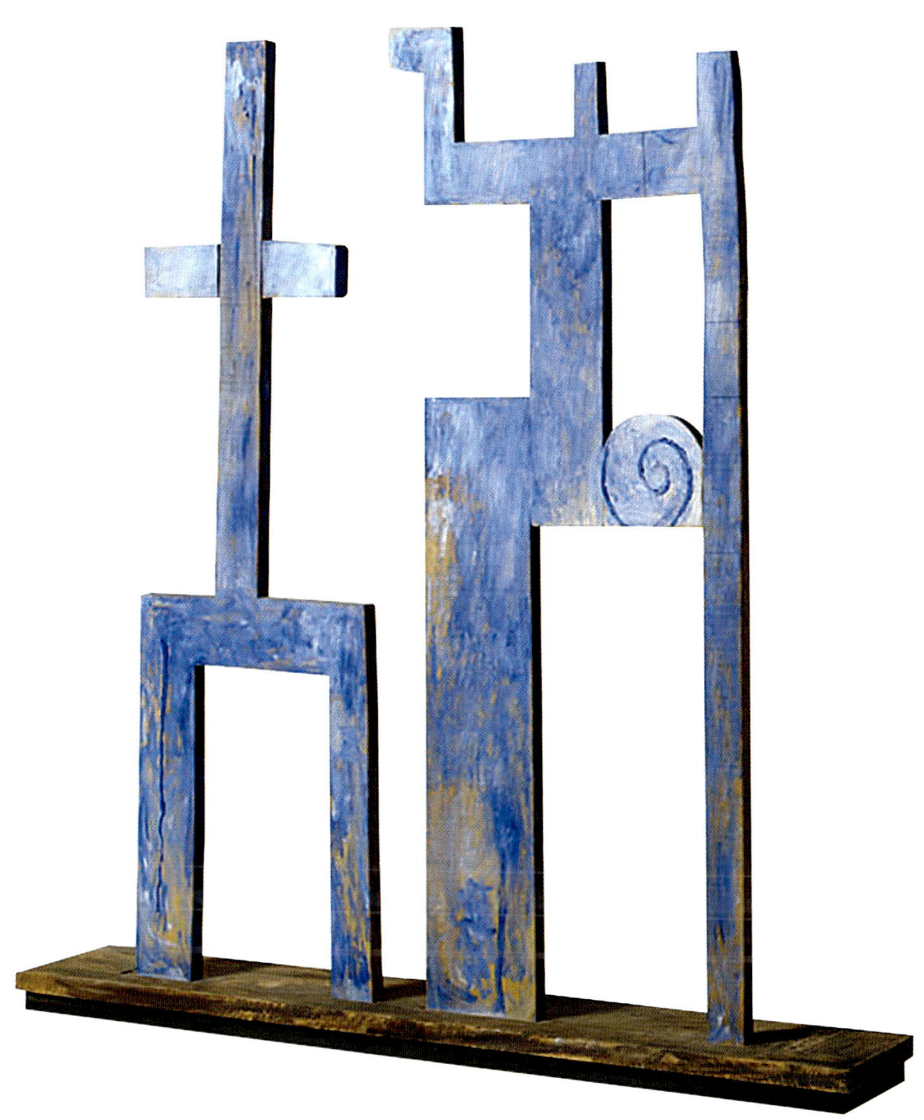

51   Monumento azul [Blue Monument] 1992; oil on wood;
68⅞ × 68⅞ × 11¾ inches. Collection Frank Ribelin.
Photo: Frank White.

Caritas

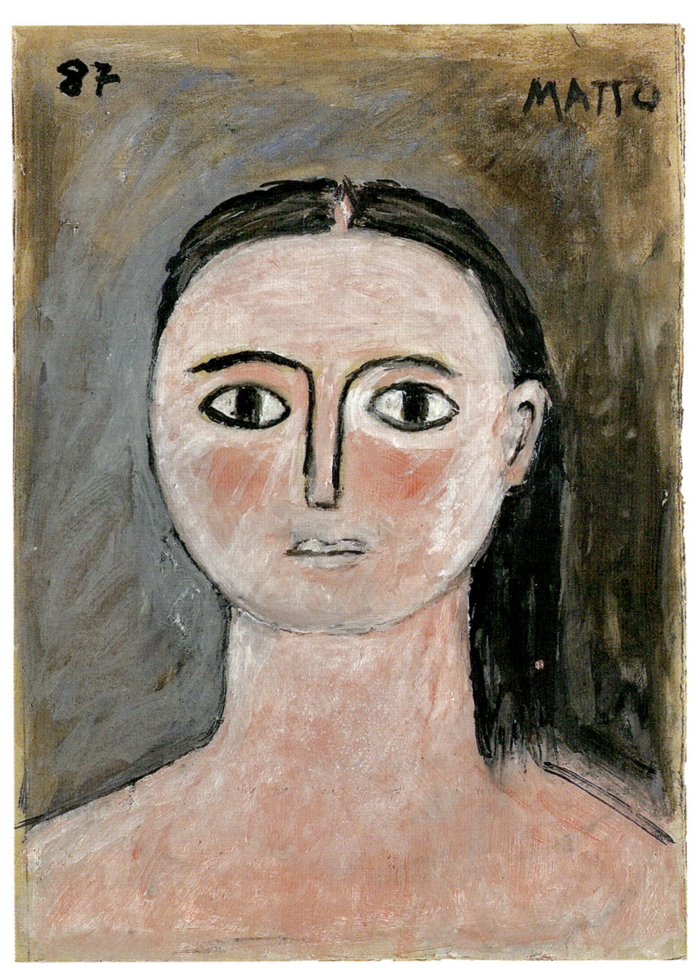

52 Carita—Hombros desnudos [Carita—Bare Shoulders] 1987; oil on cardboard; 13¾ × 9¼ inches. Collection Estate of the Artist, Courtesy of Cecilia de Torres, Ltd. Photo: Arturo Sánchez.

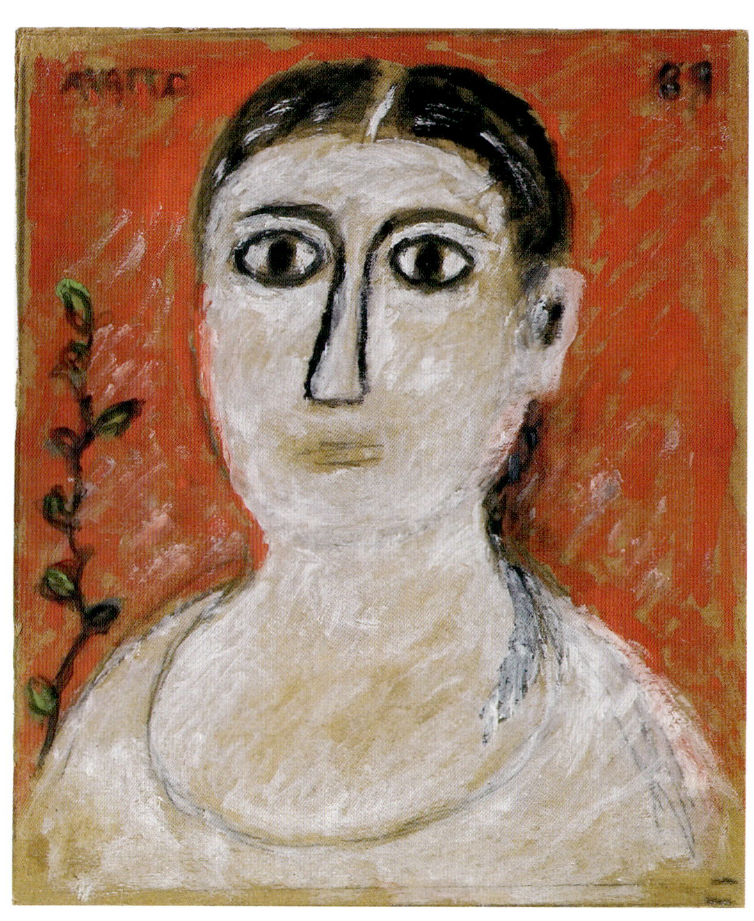

53   Carita—Hedera sobre rojo [Carita—Ivy Leaves over Red] 1989; oil on cardboard; 10⅝ × 9⅛ inches. Collection Estate of the Artist, Courtesy of Cecilia de Torres, Ltd. Photo: Arturo Sánchez.

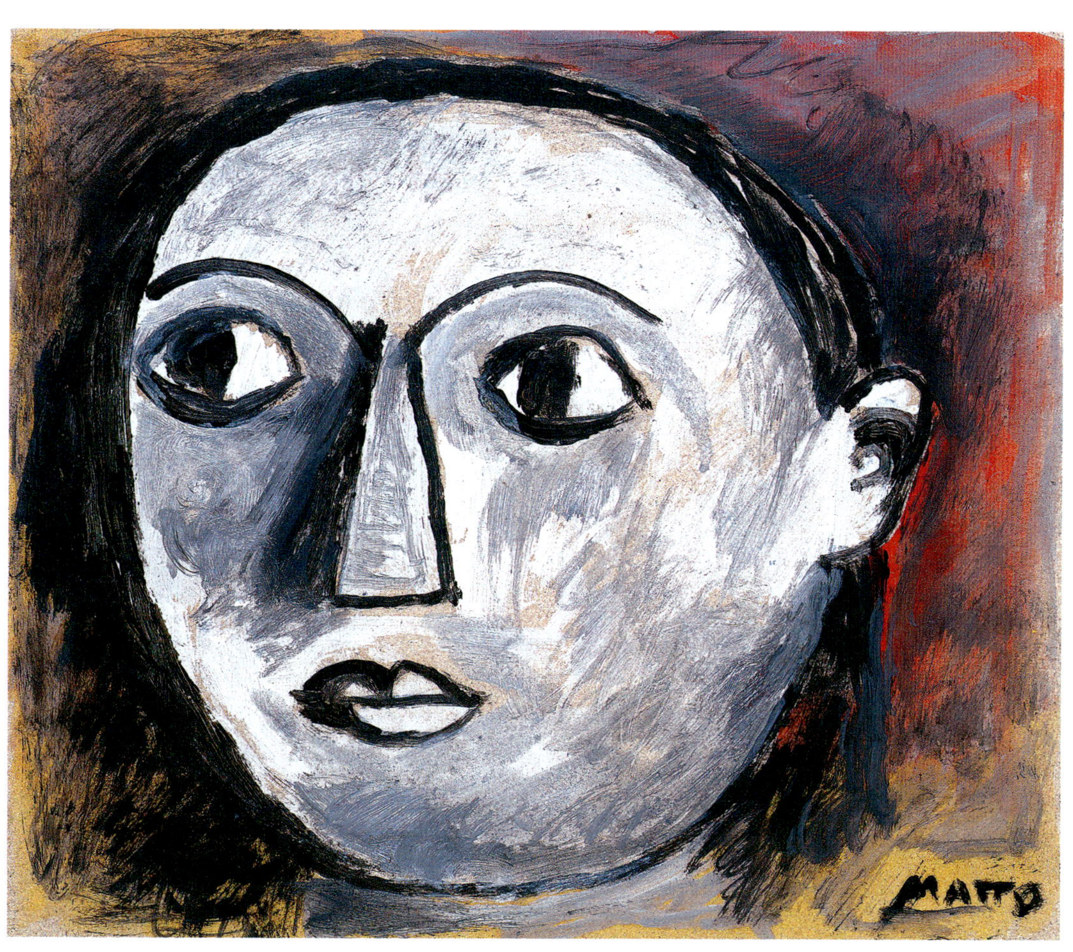

54 Carita—Perfil ¾ [Carita—¾ Profile] c. 1990; oil on cardboard;
9⅝ × 11⅜ inches. Collection Estate of the Artist, Courtesy of
Cecilia de Torres, Ltd. Photo: Larry Lamay.

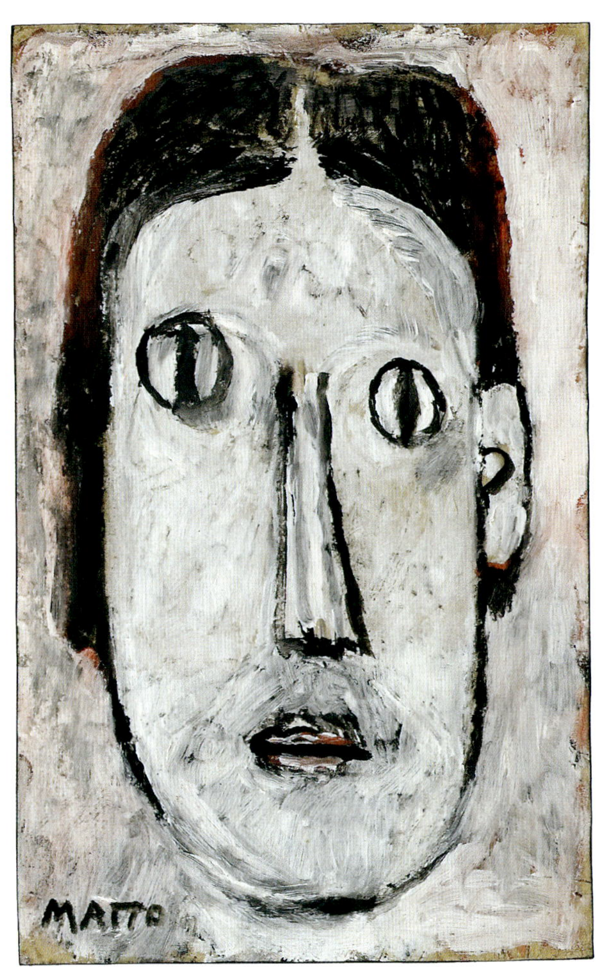

55   Carita—Ojos de gato [Carita—Cat's Eyes] 1990; oil on cardboard; 15¼ × 9¾ inches. Collection Estate of the Artist, Courtesy of Cecilia de Torres, Ltd. Photo: Arturo Sánchez.

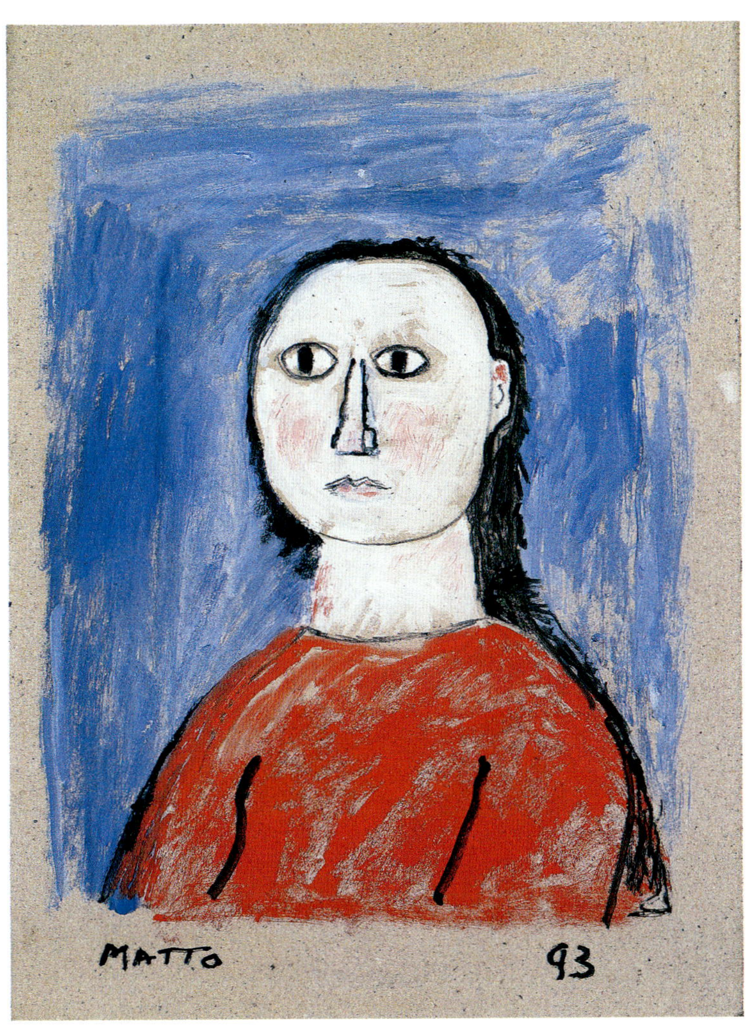

56   Carita—Vestido rojo [Carita—Red Dress] 1993; oil on cardboard; 16⅞ × 13 inches. Collection Estate of the Artist, Courtesy of Cecilia de Torres, Ltd. Photo: Larry Lamay.

FRANCISCO ALBERTO MATTO VILARÓ
(1911–1995)

Born in Montevideo, Uruguay, in 1911. He never attended school but was educated at home by tutors and studied sketching and painting with Carlos Rúfalo. At age twenty-one, he purchased baskets from the Onas tribe and his first pieces of Native American art, showing an interest in pre-Columbian art that would later influence his career. In 1962 his collection was turned into the Museo de Arte Precolombino. Matto began to paint on irregularly shaped boards; the themes were religious, an interest that would remain throughout his life. His career took a turn in 1939 when he met Joaquín Torres-García. Together they founded the Taller Torres-García in 1942. The following year he wrote *Carta pictórica: la geometría en el arte moderno* [*A Pictorial Letter: Geometry in Modern Art*] (unpublished), a book that foretells an important change in his work. His diverse individual shows include: *Francisco Matto: Elemental Forms, 1946–1993*, Galería Ramis Barquet, New York (2005); *Francisco Matto: Poesías y Pinturas 1935–1945*, Galería Oscar Prato, Montevideo (2003) and *Matto: Totems, Portraits and Graphisms*, Cecilia de Torres Ltd., New York (1999). Some of his works have appeared in group shows, including: *Modernism in Montevideo, New York and Buenos Aires: 1930s–1970s*, Cecilia de Torres Ltd. (2002); I Bienal do Mercosul, Porto Alegre, Brazil (1997); *Heterotopias*, Museo Reina Sofía, Madrid (2000); *Le Cercle de Torres-García*, Zabriskie Gallery, Paris (1996); and XV São Paulo Biennial (1979). The following are just some of the museums that include his work: Museo Nacional de Artes Plásticas y Visuales, Montevideo; Blanton Museum of Art, The University of Texas at Austin; and Museo de Bellas Artes, Caracas.

Francisco Matto, c. 1944.
Photo: Anatole Saderman.

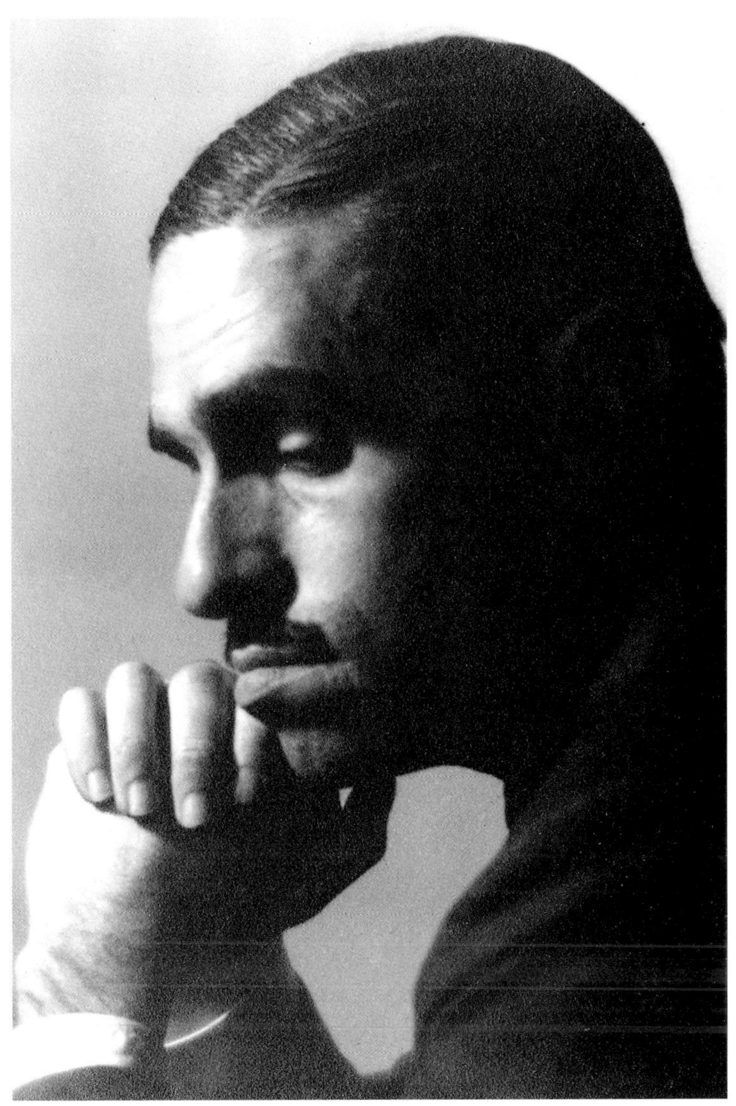

1911

Francisco Alberto Matto Vilaró was born in Montevideo on October 18. His father, Francisco Alejo Matto Vilaró, was musically inclined and his mother, María Eulalia Vilaró, wrote poetry. His brother, Jorge, died at age eight and his younger sister, Graciela, died in 1945.

1922

Matto wrote his first poems and took painting lessons with the Uruguayan painter Carlos Rúfalo. He was privately tutored at home.

1926

His father died.

1932

Traveled to Tierra del Fuego in southern Argentina and Chile where he purchased the first pieces of what would become an important collection of pre-Columbian art.

1935

Composed poems and painted Surrealist murals on the walls of his studio. Through his friends the French-Uruguayan poet Jules Supervielle and Susana Soca, met Henri Michaux, who spent the year 1936 in Uruguay.

1938

Painted large irregularly shaped wood panels such as *Mujer y gallo* [*Woman and Rooster*].

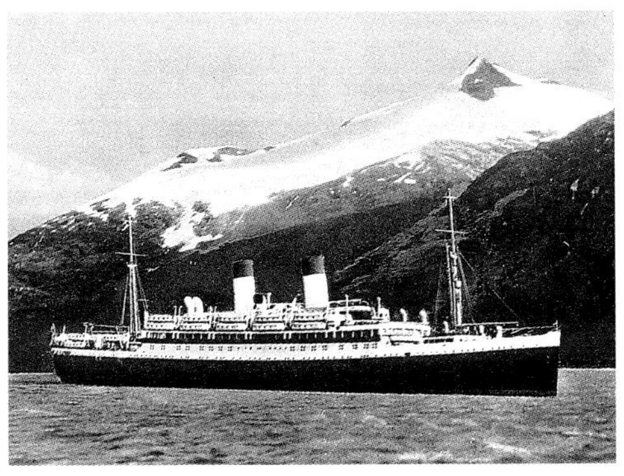

Ship in which Francisco Matto traveled to southern Argentina, 1932. Courtesy Cecilia de Torres, Ltd.

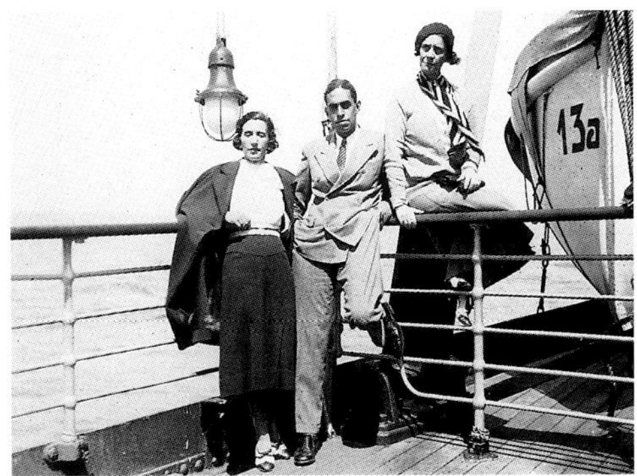

Francisco Matto and travel companions, Hortensia Vilaró and Mrs. Herman, on board a ship to southern Argentina, 1932. Courtesy Cecilia de Torres, Ltd.

1939

Met Torres-García and began to attend his lectures.

1940

Submitted two paintings, *Retrato de J.M.V.* [*Portrait of J.M.V.*] and *Guerra* [*War*] to the I Municipal Salon. In the IV National Salon, he exhibited *Mujer con vestido a rayas* [*Woman in a Striped Dress*] and *Un rincón en el parque* [*A Corner in the Park*].

1941

Exhibited *Caín y Abel* [*Cain and Abel*] at the II Municipal Salon and *La silla roja* [*The Red Chair*] at the V National Salon.

1942

With Augusto and Horacio Torres and Alceu and Edgardo Ribeiro, Matto was a founding member of the Taller Torres-García. From then on until the TTG's demise, he participated in all of the Taller Torres-García group exhibitions. Exhibited at Amigos del Arte with Augusto and Horacio Torres.

1943

He wrote *Carta pictórica: la geometría en el arte moderno* [*Pictorial Letter: Geometry in Modern Art*], unpublished, that foretold the important changes that his work would undergo. In spite of the title that refers to geometry, the text is illustrated with figures on a beach. The literary style is remarkably different from his previous writings that were filled with Surrealist and Symbolist metaphors.

René D'Harnoncourt, traveling in South America for The Museum of Modern Art, New York, visited the Taller Torres-García and Matto's studio. Returning to New York he wrote to the director of the Inter-American Bureau of Information in Montevideo, expressing his interest in purchasing for MOMA Matto's *Tres damas españolas* [*Three Spanish Ladies*], an oil on wood panel dated 1941. Matto declined to sell the work. In June the Argentine literary magazine *Verde Memoria* published an issue dedicated to Uruguayan poetry, which included Matto's *Ode to Lampeao* and poems by Mario Benedetti.

Matto wrote an essay (unpublished) in the third person about how his painting changed that year: "Towards 1945, Torres-García's influence is more evident. The accent on the vertical and horizontal and the metaphysical component in his work caused great impact on Matto. Furthermore, studying the pre-Columbian pieces from the Altiplano changed his perspective; both Torres-García and Amerindian art led him [Matto] to develop a markedly orthogonal order in his compositions and a synthetic and frontal style of painting."

In April the VII National Salon awarded prizes to Torres-García, Manuel Rosé, Gonzalo Fonseca, Lincoln Presno, and Matto, who submitted a painting titled *Harbor Scene*, which is now in the collection of the Museo Municipal de Bellas Artes Juan Manuel Blanes. Torres-García suggested that Matto join the other Taller´s artists studying painting and Constructivism. Painted abstracted geometric still lifes in primary colors.

Wrote and illustrated *Variantes formales y decorativas de las cerámicas de Tiahuanaco* [*Formal and Decorative Variants in Tiahuanaco Ceramics*], a study of the pieces in his collection. Interpreted by a contemporary artist as artworks rather than as anthropological examples. The original manuscript is in the Getty Research Foundation.

Matto made his first wood construction reliefs and drawings for large scale outdoor sculptures.

He conceived a project that was never realized, to build an artist's community in Belastiquí on the Río Santa Lucía. A series of his drawings illustrate buildings and sculptures of brick that would be made and fired on site. Each artist would design his or her own studio and monuments, creating a unified architectural environment. On August 8, Torres-García died.

1950

First trip to Europe; in Paris he met Paul Rivet, director of the Musée d'Etnographie du Trocadéro.

1952

Contributed a work for reproduction in *Treinta dibujos constructivistas* [*Thirty Constructive Drawings*], published by the Taller Torres-García.

1953

Five paintings by Matto and other works by artists of the Taller Torres-García were part of the Uruguayan presentation at the II São Paulo Biennial.

1954

Married Ada Antuña Zumarán. They traveled to Europe and Egypt. The architect Mario Paysé Reyes commissioned a brick relief for his home in Santander Street in Carrasco, a suburb of Montevideo. Paul Rivet, director of the Musée d'Etnographie du Trocadéro (Musée de L'Homme), visited Matto's collection of pre-Columbian art.

1955

While Julio Alpuy traveled abroad, Matto took over the painting classes at the Taller Torres-García that Alpuy had led since 1945.

1958

Matto again traveled to Europe, this time he visited Sicily.

1960

Designed an adobe mural relief and a stained glass window for the high school building in Las Piedras, a town near Montevideo.

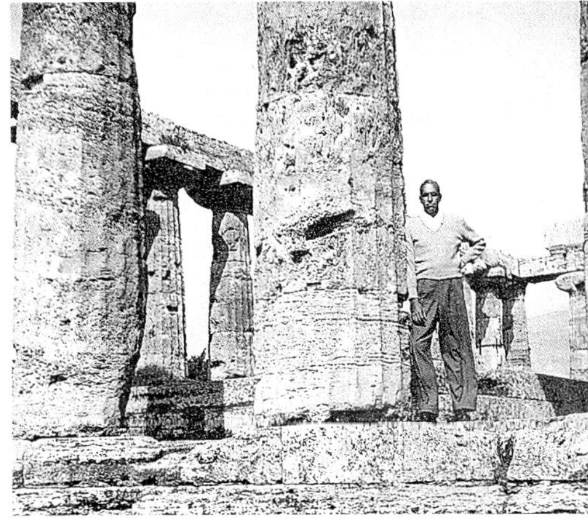

Francisco Matto in Sicily, c. 1958.
Courtesy Cecilia de Torres, Ltd.

The building also features murals by other members of the Taller Torres-García. Made his first wood *Totems.*

1962

Matto opened his collection of Amerindian art to the public. The Museo de Arte Precolombino (Museum of Pre-Columbian Art) housed ceramics, textiles, and sculpture from Argentina, Bolivia, Brazil, Chile, Colombia, Ecuador, Mexico, Peru, and Venezuela. The architect Ernesto Leborgne designed the installation, and Raúl Campá Soler did the archeological research. The photographs for the collection catalogue were by Alfredo Testoni, and the text by Esther de Cáceres. In it she explained, "The works themselves (without any archeological or ethnographic information) tell of what is essential and transcendental about them. This is a museum created by an artist, who knows that looking at art is a direct, silent, and personal experience that will shape the inner self beyond the cultural or intellectual effect." *Marcha*, a weekly newspaper, quoted Matto's comment on the works in his collection: "These art works have a continuity that reaches from their origin to the present. Modernism is unavoidably linked to these great pieces from America's past."

1965

For the garden of his friend the architect Ernesto Leborgne, Matto designed three works: a mural in gray stone and marble (p. 20) named *Homenaje a Lautréamont* after the French poet born in Montevideo, a Constructivist cut-brick relief, and a Constructivist carving in limestone.

1966

Carlos Gradín of *La Prensa* in Buenos Aires published a review of Matto's museum, February 27.

1967

In Hamburg the magazine *Humboldt* n.29 reproduced several pre-Columbian pieces from Matto's collection.

1968

Matto's Museo de Arte Precolombino presented an exhibition of eighty-eight objects of diverse Amerindian origin titled *The Figure of the American Man*, organized by Ernesto Leborgne and Matto. They published an illustrated catalogue with a text by José María Montero Pérez. The museum also organized an exhibition of African art, with eighty-two pieces from the collections of the Taller Torres-García artists and their friends.

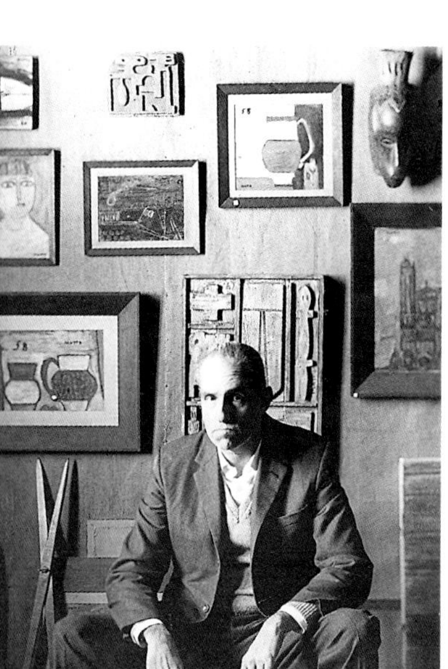

Francisco Matto in his studio, c. 1966.
Courtesy Cecilia de Torres, Ltd.

The Central Bank of Uruguay commissioned Matto to design a silver coin for the FAO (United Nations Organization for Agriculture and Food). Ernesto Leborgne made the plaster cast and the Casa de la Moneda in Chile minted the coin. In Uruguay it was put in general circulation and was worth 1000 pesos.

Traveled to New York for the opening of Torres-García's retrospective exhibition at the Solomon R. Guggenheim Museum. Visited Mexico and Peru.

The international numismatic association Gesellschaft Für Internationale Geldgeschichte with headquarters in Germany awarded that year's first prize to Matto's coin.

Traveled to Europe and the United States. Exhibited at Galería Monzón, Madrid.

To celebrate Torres-García's centenary, the Museo de Arte Precolombino organized an exhibition and published an illustrated catalogue of Torres-García's wood constructions and toys.

The municipal government withdrew its modest support of the Museo de Arte Precolombino, and Matto was forced to close it. It has remained closed ever since, even though in 1998 Matto's widow donated the collection to the city of Montevideo. Painted the first series of simplified faces inspired by early Christian painting.

Matto designed a wrought iron window grill for the house of the architect Rafael Lorente Escudero in Carrasco, a suburb of Montevideo.

Matto was invited to participate in the Primer Encuentro Internacional de Escultura Moderna al Aire Libre (First International Meeting for Modern Open-Air Sculpture) in Punta del Este, a project of sculptures for public spaces. The participants were: from Argentina, Gyula Kosice, Enio Iommi, and Jacques Bedel; from

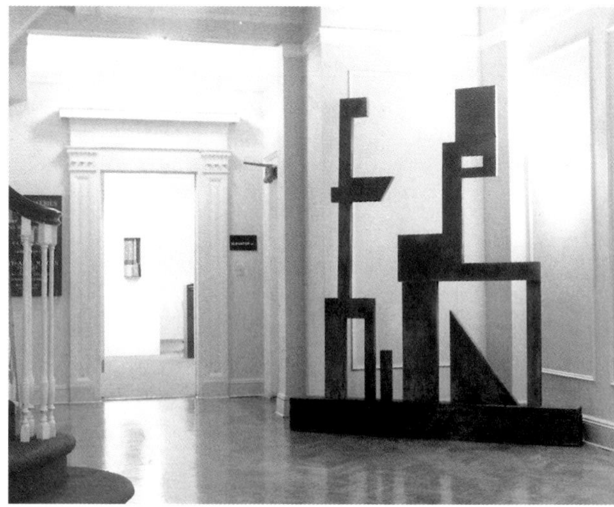

Francisco Matto's *Formas en azul [Forms in Blue]*, 1979, as installed at the exhibition *Torres-García and His Legacy*, Kouros Gallery, New York, 1986. Courtesy Cecilia de Torres, Ltd.

Brazil, Waltercio Caldas; from Colombia, Edgar Negret; from Chile, Mario Irarrazabal; from Paraguay, Herman Guggiari; and from Uruguay, Nelson Ramos and Matto. He designed a three-meter high U-shaped form in cement that still stands on the shoreline.

1985

Traveled to New York for the opening of the exhibition *Torres-García and His Legacy* at the Kouros Gallery. This was his last trip abroad.

1991

Involved himself in the production and design of the catalogue *Matto, Painting and Sculpture*, text by Anhelo Hernández, photos by Alfredo Testoni and Daniela Chappard.

1995

Matto died on September 15, nearly 84. Anhelo Hernández wrote, "Matto wasn't fond of theorizing, when someone did, he started to whistle an air by Bach or to praise Stravinsky. But that didn't prevent him from elaborating the clear and concise thoughts that guided him. Matto wrote, 'If we succeed in creating elemental forms, we will achieve the understanding of mystery.'"

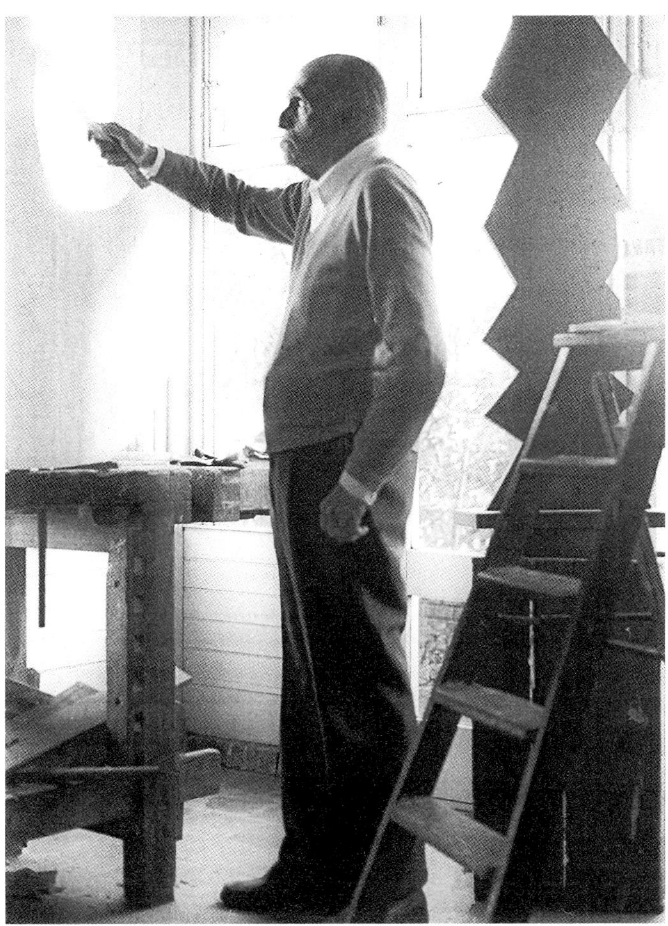

Francisco Matto preparing his model for *Forma* [*Form*],
the "U" sculpture, c. 1982. Courtesy Cecilia de Torres, Ltd.

Exhibition Checklist

Francisco Matto, c. 1948
Oil on canvas
32¾ × 26¾ inches
Collection Ada Antuña de Matto,
Montevideo

Naturaleza muerta [Still Life], 1945
Oil on cardboard on canvas
21¾ × 33⅜ inches
Collection Judy and Charles Tate, Houston

Naturaleza muerta constructivo [Constructive
Still Life], 1946
Oil on canvas
23⅝ × 27⅞ inches
Collection Estate of the Artist, Courtesy
of Cecilia de Torres, Ltd.

Perspectiva Ciudad Vieja [Perspective of Ciudad
Vieja], 1946
Oil on cardboard on canvas
31½ × 41¼ inches
Private collection

Pintura constructiva [Constructive Painting],
1946
Oil on cardboard
20½ × 24¼ inches
Collection Estate of the Artist, Courtesy
of Cecilia de Torres, Ltd.

Naturaleza muerta con plano de color y línea
[Still Life with Color Plane and Line], c. 1947
Oil on cardboard
19½ × 25⅞ inches
Collection Estate of the Artist, Courtesy
of Cecilia de Torres, Ltd.

Dos dibujos [Two Drawings], c. 1948
Pencil and watercolor on paper
7⅛ × 5⅛ inches
Collection Estate of the Artist, Courtesy
of Cecilia de Torres, Ltd.

Dibujo para una escultura [Study for a
Sculpture], 1950–1988
Ink and crayon on paper
6½ × 8 inches
Collection Estate of the Artist, Courtesy
of Cecilia de Torres, Ltd.

Composición con seis compartimentos
[Composition with Six Compartments], 1950
Oil on board
15 × 20 inches
Collection Frank Ribelin

Puerto en colores primarios [Port in Primary
Colors], 1950
Oil on cardboard
20¾ × 31½ inches
Collection Daniela Chappard Foundation

Constructivo con reloj [Constructive with Clock],
1951
Oil on cardboard on canvas
26⅝ × 19⅞ inches
Collection Galería Oscar Prato, Montevideo

Paisaje del puerto [Port Landscape], 1951
Oil on canvas
19¾ × 23⅝ inches
Collection Galería Oscar Prato, Montevideo

Dos dibujos [Two Sketches], 1952
Pencil, watercolor, and ink on paper
13⅝ × 8¾ inches
Collection Estate of the Artist, Courtesy
of Cecilia de Torres, Ltd.

Sol y formas [Sun and Forms], 1952
Oil on cardboard
14 × 21 inches
Private collection, Houston

Naturaleza muerta con jarra [Still Life with Jar],
1955
Oil on cardboard
12⅝ × 16½ inches
Collection Ada Antuña de Matto,
Montevideo

Geniol, 1956
Oil on cardboard
12¼ × 18¾ inches
Collection Estate of the Artist, Courtesy
of Cecilia de Torres, Ltd.

Estructura en azul, blanco y rojo [Blue, White,
and Red Structure], c. 1957
Oil on board on canvas
35⅛ × 40¾ inches
Private collection, Montevideo

Perspectiva [Perspective], 1957
Oil on cardboard
16⅛ × 21¾ inches
Collection Ada Antuña de Matto,
Montevideo

Composición sobre fondo negro [Composition on
Black Background], 1958
Oil on cardboard
15 × 18 inches
Blanton Museum of Art, The University of
Texas at Austin, Gift of Judy and Charles
Tate, 2004.172

Naturaleza muerta [Still Life], 1958
Oil on cardboard
13 × 18⅛ inches
Private collection

Dos formas [Two Forms], 1959
Oil on wood
41¼ × 31⅞ inches
Collection Daniela Chappard Foundation

Removedor—Relieve [Removedor—Relief],
1959
Oil on wood
15 × 20⅞ inches
Collection Estate of the Artist, Courtesy
of Cecilia de Torres, Ltd.

Barcos [Boats], c. 1960
Oil on cardboard
18¾ × 15 inches
Collection Ada Antuña de Matto,
Montevideo

Retícula blanco y negro [Big Black and
White Grid], 1960
Oil on wood
55 × 70½ inches
Collection Estate of the Artist, Courtesy
of Cecilia de Torres, Ltd.

Construcción en madera [Construction in Wood],
c. 1960
Oil on wood
23¼ × 24¼ inches
Private collection, Miami

Constructivo Nueva York [Constructive New
York], 1960
Oil on cardboard
40⅞ × 31¼ inches
Collection Estate of the Artist, Courtesy
of Cecilia de Torres, Ltd.

Dos formas en rojo [Two Forms in Red], 1960
Pencil and watercolor on paper
5¾ × 3¾ inches
Collection Estate of the Artist, Courtesy
of Cecilia de Torres, Ltd.

Flecha blanca [White Arrow], 1960
Oil on wood
23¼ × 35⅜ inches
Collection Estate of the Artist, Courtesy
of Cecilia de Torres, Ltd.

Flecha blanca [White Arrow], c. 1960
Watercolor on paper
6¾ × 7⅞ inches
Collection Estate of the Artist, Courtesy
of Cecilia de Torres, Ltd.

Puerto con cielo rojo [Port with Red Sky], 1960
Oil on canvas
19¾ × 27⅝ inches
Collection Estate of the Artist, Courtesy
of Cecilia de Torres, Ltd.

Serpiente [Snake], 1960
Oil on wood
84¼ × 8¾ × 7½ inches
Collection Estate of the Artist, Courtesy
of Cecilia de Torres, Ltd.

Constructivo octubre 1911 [Constructive October
1911], 1962
Oil on cardboard
40⅞ × 27¾ inches
Collection Mary Lile, Houston,
Courtesy of Cecilia de Torres, Ltd.

Constructivo sin color [Colorless Constructive],
1962
Ink and pencil on paper
8½ × 11 inches
Collection Estate of the Artist, Courtesy
of Cecilia de Torres, Ltd.

Rejilla en amarillo y azul [Grid in Yellow and
Blue], 1962
Magic marker on paper
15 × 11 inches
Collection Estate of the Artist, Courtesy
of Cecilia de Torres, Ltd.

Construcción en cinco colores [Construction in Five Colors], 1963
Oil and graphite on cloth
43¾ × 25⅜ inches
Collection Judy and Charles Tate, Houston

Rayo [Lightning], 1963
Oil on wood
25¼ × 4⅛ × 2¼ inches
Collection Galería Oscar Prato, Montevideo

Sol [Sun], 1963
Oil on wood
23¾ × 23¾ inches
Private collection, Washington, D.C.

Construcción redonda [Round Construction], 1965–1980
Oil on wood
52⅜ × 52⅜ × 3½ inches
Collection Daniela Chappard Foundation

Monumento en quebracho [Monument in Quebracho Wood], c. 1965
Wood
55⅞ × 44⅞ × 7½ inches
Private collection

Diez formas [Ten Forms], 1966
Wood relief
28 × 12⅜ inches
Private collection, New York, Courtesy of Cecilia de Torres, Ltd.

Cinco formas [Five Forms], 1967
Oil on cardboard
35⅝ × 44 inches
Collection Lauren and Jeffrey Sugar

Ideas, 1967
Oil on fiberboard
28 × 40 inches
Private collection

Constructivo rosa con caracol [Rose Constructive with Snail], 1967
Oil on cardboard
33⅛ × 33½ inches
Collection Estate of the Artist, Courtesy of Cecilia de Torres, Ltd.

Naturaleza muerta planista con botella y jarra [Planar Still Life with Bottle and Jar], 1967
Oil on cardboard on canvas
16¾ × 22 inches
Collection Galería Oscar Prato, Montevideo

Constructivo con máscara [Constructive with Mask], c. 1968
Oil on wood
36⅜ × 29¾ inches
Private collection, Montevideo

Dibujo para un monumento [Study for a Monument], c. 1970
Pencil on paper
17¼ × 13¾ inches
Collection Estate of the Artist, Courtesy of Cecilia de Torres, Ltd.

U, 1970
Oil on wood
84 inches (height)
Collection Susan and Mac Dunwoody, Houston

Forma blanca [White Form], c. 1970
Oil on wood
56¼ × 37½ inches
Private collection, New York, Courtesy of Cecilia de Torres, Ltd.

Untitled, 1971
Oil on wood
16⅞ × 12⅝ inches
Collection Daniela Chappard Foundation

Formas [Forms], 1974
Oil on canvas
61 × 57⅞ inches
Private collection

Veleta [Wind Vane], 1974
Oil on canvas
21⅜ × 17⅝ inches
Collection Estate of the Artist, Courtesy of Cecilia de Torres, Ltd.

Construcción en blanco y celeste—Relieve [Construction in White and Sky Blue—Relief], 1975
Oil on wood
23¼ × 13⅜ inches
Collection Estate of the Artist, Courtesy of Cecilia de Torres, Ltd.

Dos Venus [Two Venuses], 1976
Oil on wood
44⅞ × 26⅜ × 6¾ inches
Collection Estate of the Artist, Courtesy of Cecilia de Torres, Ltd.

Elementos amarillos [Yellow Elements], c. 1978
China ink and watercolor on paper
4⅛ × 6¼ inches
Collection Estate of the Artist, Courtesy of Cecilia de Torres, Ltd.

Construcción [Construction], 1979
Oil on wood
52 × 35⅜ × 7⅞ inches
Collection Estate of the Artist, Courtesy of Cecilia de Torres, Ltd.

Cordero [Lamb], c. 1979
Oil on wood
70¼ × 15½ × 4¾ inches
The Museum of Fine Arts, Houston, Gift of Ada Antuña de Matto

Formas proyecto de monumento [Project for Monument Forms], 1979
Pencil, crayon, and watercolor on paper
8½ × 8½ inches
Collection Estate of the Artist, Courtesy of Cecilia de Torres, Ltd.

Máscara [Mask], 1979
Oil on wood
82½ × 9¼ × 5¾ inches
The Museum of Fine Arts, Houston, Gift of Alfred C. Glassell III and Marli Andrade, Mary and Roy Cullen, Marjorie H. Wortham, Joanna and Richard W. Wortham III, and the Caroline Wiess Law Foundation

Monumento [Monument], 1979
Oil on wood
89⅜ × 83½ × 13¾ inches
Private collection

Venus rosa [Rose Venus], 1979
Oil on wood
81⅞ inches (height)
Collection Susan and Mac Dunwoody, Houston

Venus, 1979
Oil on wood
82 × 10¾ × 10 inches
The Museum of Fine Arts, Houston,
Gift of Alfred C. Glassell III and
Marli Andrade, Mary and Roy Cullen,
Marjorie H. Wortham, Joanna and
Richard W. Wortham III, and the
Caroline Wiess Law Foundation

Venus blanquiazul [White and Blue Venus],
1980
Oil on wood
96 × 13¾ × 12 inches
The Museum of Fine Arts, Houston,
Gift of Alfred C. Glassell III and
Marli Andrade, Mary and Roy Cullen,
Marjorie H. Wortham, Joanna and
Richard W. Wortham III, and the
Caroline Wiess Law Foundation

Pareja [Couple], c. 1982
Marble
19⁵⁄₁₆ × 25⁹⁄₁₆ inches
Colección Patricia Phelps de Cisneros

Constructivo [Constructive], 1983
Oil on cardboard
39 × 31⅛ inches
Private collection, Montevideo

Constructivo América [America Constructive],
1983
Oil on cardboard on canvas
23 × 28⅛ inches
Collection Galería Oscar Prato, Montevideo

Caracol grande [Large Snail], 1985
Oil on wood
64 × 12 × 10 inches
The Museum of Fine Arts, Houston,
Gift of Alfred C. Glassell III and
Marli Andrade, Mary and Roy Cullen,
Marjorie H. Wortham, Joanna and
Richard W. Wortham III, and the
Caroline Wiess Law Foundation

Carita—Hombros desnudos [Carita—
Bare Shoulders], 1987
Oil on cardboard
13¾ × 9¼ inches
Collection Estate of the Artist, Courtesy
of Cecilia de Torres, Ltd.

Hombre universal [Universal Man], 1988
Oil on wood
83 inches (height)
Collection Estate of the Artist, Courtesy of
Cecilia de Torres, Ltd.

Dintel [Lintel], 1988
Oil on wood
24 × 3¾ × 3¾ inches
Collection Judy and Charles Tate, Houston

Carita—Hedera sobre rojo [Carita—Ivy Leaves
over Red], 1989
Oil on cardboard
10⅝ × 9⅛ inches
Collection Estate of the Artist, Courtesy
of Cecilia de Torres, Ltd.

Serpiente [Snake], 1989
Oil on wood
24 × 3¾ × 3¾ inches
Collection Galería Oscar Prato, Montevideo

Carita—Ojos de gato [Carita—Cat's Eyes],
1990
Oil on cardboard
15¼ × 9¾ inches
Collection Estate of the Artist, Courtesy
of Cecilia de Torres, Ltd.

Carita—Perfil ¾ [Carita—¾ Profile], c. 1990
Oil on cardboard
9⅝ × 11⅜ inches
Collection Estate of the Artist, Courtesy
of Cecilia de Torres, Ltd.

Monumento azul [Blue Monument], 1992
Oil on wood
68⅞ × 68⅞ × 11¾ inches
Collection Frank Ribelin

Carita—Vestido rojo [Carita—Red Dress], 1993
Oil on cardboard
16⅞ × 13 inches
Collection Estate of the Artist, Courtesy
of Cecilia de Torres, Ltd.

Azul y blanco [Blue and White], n.d.
Oil on wood
91¼ inches (height)
Collection Susan and Mac Dunwoody,
Houston

Lenders to the Exhibition

Institutions

Blanton Museum of Art, The University of Texas at Austin
Colección Patricia Phelps de Cisneros
Daniela Chappard Foundation
Museum of Fine Arts, Houston

Galleries

Cecilia de Torres, Ltd., New York
Galería Oscar Prato, Montevideo
Sicardi Gallery, Houston

Private Collections

Ada Antuña de Matto
Susan and Mac Dunwoody
Mary Lile
Frank Ribelin
Lauren and Jeffrey Sugar
Judy and Charles Tate